A GUIDE TO
JEWISH PRACTICE

ETHICS
OF SPEECH

A GUIDE
to JEWISH
PRACTICE

Center for Jewish Ethics
Reconstructionist Rabbinical College
in cooperation with the
Reconstructionist Rabbinical Association

Reconstructionist Rabbinical College Press

1299 Church Road, Wyncote, PA 19095-1898
www.rrc.edu

ETHICS
OF SPEECH

DAVID A. TEUTSCH

Reconstructionist Rabbinical College Press
Wyncote, Pennsylvania

Composition by G&H Soho, Inc.

ISBN 0-938945-11-4

2005935343

Printed in the U.S.A.

Contents

Dedication

My parents, Eric and Hilda Teutsch, made Jewish living a natural part of my life. Their support and commitment to education laid the foundation for my work.

The challenge of addressing the questions raised by my children, Zachary and Nomi, has sharpened my thinking about these issues. Their love and support and that of my wife, Betsy, have sustained my efforts.

The support of friends and colleagues was invaluable, both as I developed the methods for this project and as my work proceeded.

To my family, friends and colleagues, this book is dedicated.

David A. Teutsch

Commentators

Joshua Boettiger (J.B.)

Barbara E. Breitman (B.E.B.)

Dan Ehrenkrantz (D.E.)

Michael Fessler (M.F.)

Shai Gluskin (S.J.G.)

Chayim Herzig-Marx (C.H-M.)

Richard Hirsh (R.H.)

Leah Kamionkowski (L.K.)

Tamar Kamionkowski (T.K.)

Seth F. Kreimer (S.F.K.)

Darby J. Leigh (D.J.L.)

Nina H.Mandel (N.H.M)

Vivie Mayer (V.M.)

Deborah Dash Moore (D.D.M.)

Joyce Norden (J.N.)

Yael Ridberg (Y.R.)

Dennis C. Sasso (D.C.S.)

Jacob J. Staub (J.J.S.)

Robert P. Tabak (R.P.T.)

Sheila Peltz Weinberg (S.P.W.)

Advisory Committee

Rabbis Richard Hirsh and David Teutsch, *Co-chairs*

Rabbi Lester Bronstein

Deborah Dash Moore, Ph.D.

Chayim Herzig-Marx

Leah Kamionkowski

Rabbi Nina Mandel

Rabbi Yael Ridberg

Rabbi Jacob Staub

Preface

The way we use speech can build or destroy our communities. Language may be the most powerful single tool that contemporary people have. This volume provides a moral framework for using that tool.

This fifth section of *A Guide to Jewish Practice* completes one more step of the enormous undertaking of producing a comprehensive, values-based guide for contemporary Jews. The project continues to gather momentum.

The efforts and support of the *Guide's* Advisory Committee and of the commentators are critical to the success of this project. Their advice has substantially improved the text, but all remaining faults are mine. Cheryl Plumly has again faithfully typed the drafts of the manuscript. Gerry Cohen and Lauren Handel helped with technical aspects of production, and Jim Harris and his team at G & H Soho, Inc., did the typesetting and production.

This volume and my work on it have been funded by the Levin-Lieber Program in Jewish Ethics of the Reconstructionist Rabbinical College. I am grateful to Dan Levin for his ongoing support.

David A. Teutsch

ETHICS
OF SPEECH

According to Genesis, God brought the world into being by speaking. Speech has been described as the "holiest of the holy" (*Igeret HaGra,* written by the Vilna Gaon in the 18th century). Jewish tradition teaches that "life and death lie in the power of the tongue" (Proverbs

In Genesis 1, God brings the world into being through speaking, differentiating and naming. Giving a word or a name to something in effect makes it real. We continue to create the world by the names we give to people and things. If we label someone as untrustworthy or self-centered, we contribute to the way that person is perceived and treated. — T.K.

The only holiday on the Jewish calendar that references the creation of the world is Rosh Hashana, called, among other names, *(ha)yom harat ha'olam,* the day of the world's birth. Just as in the Torah myth the world is brought into creation through speech, so each year on Rosh Hashana the world is recreated through acts of speech, as we offer words of apology, confession, atonement, forgiveness and reconciliation.
— R.H.

Our prayer lives constantly remind us of the power of words. The midrash (*Vayikra Raba* 33:1) tells the story of Rabban Shimon ben Gamaliel sending his servant Tabi out to buy "good" food. When Tabi comes back with a tongue to eat, Rabban Gamaliel sends him out a second time, this time for "bad" food. Again, he comes back with a tongue. The word *lashon* means both tongue and language. Tabi's point is that the power of the tongue to create speech can be used for good or ill. — J.B.

Prayer helps remind us of how high the stakes are—for good and ill—when we use our tongues to speak, and how much rests on our abilities to discern and use our powers of speech skillfully. The weekday *Amida* prayer is a testament to this. Among other things, it recognizes the damage to a community that slanderous speech (*malshinut*) can do, and pleads that our voices themselves be heard (*sh'ma kolenu*) positively. The prayer concludes with *elohay n'tzor l'shoni mera, usfatay midaber mirma*—My God, guard my tongue from evil and my lips from speaking deceitfully. We sometimes take prayer for granted, but it is fascinating that we stand before God with *words* as offerings. — J.B.

18:21). This seemingly hyperbolic statement turns out not to be an exaggeration; words have stunning power.

Language provides the primary vehicle for human beings to interpret their encounter with the world. Language plays a central role in creating the world in which we live by giving us the names, concepts and cognition that shape our consciousness. Indeed, our world is unimaginable without words. Through talking, writing, thinking, reading and listening, through books, conversations, radio, computers, television, lectures, discussions, plays and poetry, we not only

For those of us who understand the world as mediated through language, it is very difficult to imagine human existence without words. However, there are many in our society—including babies and those born with severe cognitive disability or afflicted with dementia or a serious brain injury—who are fully human even though their lives do not contain words. The veneration our tradition holds for words should not allow us to slip into a subtle devaluing of people who are unable to communicate through speech. D.E.

For some, silent meditation or a retreat where participants may be silent for weeks at a time can be a useful way to remember the awesome power of words. If attending such a retreat is unthinkable for you, try spending a single day or at least a few hours without speaking at all. Notice how the first few words, phrases and sentences feel after that. Do you give more attention to what you're saying?   — D.J.L.

The Israeli poet Yehuda Amichai wrote that the Jewish journey is the journey toward language: "Even Moses climbed Mount Sinai not as mountaineers do, but to receive the Tablets of the Law." (*Open Closed Open*, p. 117) Language is a gift. As humans we try to offer back that gift from God in our own imperfect ways. Language falls short by definition, but it is our most noble attempt. We are always learning to speak.   — J.B.

We Jews are a verbal people. Our Torah begins with the "word of God" that creates worlds: "And God said, 'Let there be light.'" Words have creative power. This is captured in the magical expression "abracadabra." This ancient Aramaic word literally means "I will create (*abra*) as I speak (*kadabra*)." Words indeed have magical powers. They can create worlds. Words can hurt or heal, soothe or irritate, seduce or alienate, make peace or proclaim war.   — D.C.S.

shape our world but are shaped by it. Language is the primary tool for creating and shaping culture and for creating the cooperation needed to accomplish tasks large and small.

Children learn to recognize different people and objects through learning their names. They learn to value themselves in part through the language with which their parents express their love. Children learn to behave in various ways through imitation and verbal instruction. The way they experience the world is fundamentally shaped by language. When they start to have relationships with peers, language provides a crucial part of the communication, and as relationships become

The technologies of inexpensive telephone service, voicemail, email, and the Web have dramatically increased the amount of speech that we encounter each day. Managing our exposure to this information is a challenge that has been likened to sipping from a fire hose. Technology has also shifted the nature of the speech we encounter. Through most of the previous century, mass media were centralized and controlled by large corporations. Innovations such as email and weblogs have radically democratized the information we are exposed to: An individual's writing can potentially reach millions, sometimes without the writer's consent. This magnification of the reach of our own speech makes attention to the ethics of speech all the more urgent.   — M.F.

Children not only learn to recognize objects through learning their names; children learn how their culture and tradition give particular names to objects that can be found in universal settings. The names we give to common objects can transform them from the mundane to the sacred, as when we name a scroll "The Torah," a shawl "*tallit,*" an amulet "mezuzah," or a canopy "ḥupa."   — R.H.

How we speak and how we listen facilitate the emergence of self or the silencing of the self. This is one way that speech creates and destroys worlds.   — B.E.B.

George Lakoff and Mark Johnson have argued that language is replete with metaphor and that metaphoric language conveys conceptual thinking on a level of which we are barely aware. Thus, our words communicate both literal meaning and subtle conceptual thinking. For example, when we say things like: "I'm a little rusty today," or "We've been working all day, and now we're running out of steam," we are conveying the metaphor that the mind is a machine. (George Lakoff and Mark Johnson, *Metaphors We Live By,* University of Chicago Press, 1980, p.27)   — T.K.

more complex and sophisticated, speech (used throughout to mean any form using words—oral, written, signed and recorded) plays an ever-growing role. Children blossom when they receive verbal encouragement and praise, and they wither when they encounter a welter of verbal negativity and criticism. While the results may not always be so immediate or obvious, that is true for adults as well.

Given the enormous power of words to create and destroy, their use is a matter of considerable moral concern. Individual conversation, group interaction and

Not all speech is spoken or written. I am referring not only to the various signed languages used around the world, but also to the myriad ways in which each of us employs non-verbal communication every day. We communicate as much or more than our words do with a tilt of the head, a shrug of the shoulders, a roll of the eyes. We also communicate volumes by what we don't say. When we don't tell someone that we're sorry, or how much we appreciate what they've done, they may conclude, rightly or wrongfully, that we're not sorry or that we take them for granted.　— D.J.L.

The Talmud is a sea of words. Medieval Jews produced philosophers, grammarians and poets. Not granted the benefit of self-rule, nor sometimes the right to own and work the land, nor permission to join the trade guilds of pre-modern Europe, we produced statesmen, international travelers and traders. Through words and ideas they helped to link and to build economies and countries where Jews were still regarded as strangers. Some civilizations have contributed great art and music to the world; others, great architecture and technology; and yet others are known as great lovers or warriors. We Jews have contributed much to all of these, but we have especially contributed ideas and words, words, words.　— D.C.S.

It has always struck me that a remarkably large proportion of the sins in the *Al Ḥet* confessional prayer in the Yom Kippur liturgy concern speech. Examining that list suggests both the variety of ways in which speech can be morally problematic and the salience that this set of sins seems to hold for the Jewish community. Legend has it that the Inuit have an extraordinary number of words for varieties of snow. In our textually and verbally impacted culture, 17 of the 44 sins enumerated in the *Al Ḥet* in my *maḥzor* explicitly involve speech. Others, such as pride and causeless hatred, can be committed by speech but need not be.　— S.F.K.

Words have three other qualities worth highlighting: 1. Words have the power to manipulate others. To the extent that we can shape others' understanding of reality,

speeches; notes and letters; essays, poetry, lyrics, plays, movies and novels; journalism and broadcasting; e-mail, chat rooms and even spam all have a substantial impact on others, to say nothing of verbal agreements, coaching, romancing—the list goes on and on. Therefore, the use of speech in its many forms raises powerful moral questions. Everyone struggles from time to time with what to say and what not to say, and with how to respond when someone

we can control their actions. This power can sometimes be used for good: Clearly and accurately explaining the context of others' situations can help them increase control over their own lives. But it can also be used immorally: By misleading others, I can bend them to my will against their own. The harm of a lie is in part that if believed, it gives the liar illegitimate control over the hearer. 2. Words have the power to create human connections. Beyond utilitarian partnerships, the creation of a shared space of meaning creates a bond. Usually this is a human good, although it can also be pathological. The bond created by joint efforts to plan a hate crime is problematic even if the crime does not come about because it both adversely affects the character of the participants and creates a connection that is likely to produce evil. At a less dramatic level, the bond created by malicious gossip may have similar effects. 3. Words have the power to define the speaker. It is not uncommon, in my life, at least, to find that I come to realize my own judgment as I express it. Equally important, speech generates understandings, traits of character and habits of thought that carry through to other actions. It is well to avoid uncharitable judgment or hateful speech, and to seek opportunities to celebrate virtue, for example, even in one's diary. God created the world by speaking; we create our inner worlds in the same fashion.   — S.F.K.

Not only do words themselves raise moral issues, but the act of effectively controlling who does and doesn't have access to words also raises moral issues. Given the centrality of language and communication, it is wrong to deprive others of access to our words just because they can't hear or they use a different language. What do we communicate about our perception of the value and worth of each individual in our audience if we don't make every attempt to ensure that everyone will have access to what we say? What do we communicate about our perception of the value and worth of every individual when we willingly expend time, energy and financial resources to ensure the presence of an American Sign Language interpreter or language translator? Many deaf people share a common experience of missing something that was said and asking to have it repeated, only to be told, "It wasn't important," or "Never mind." Perhaps it's only unimportant when you already know what was said. Being left in the dark could be the most important moment of your day.   — D.J.L.

else has said or done the wrong thing. Often we wish others had struggled a bit more before they spoke or wrote!

We live in a society that bombards us with words. They come so fast and furious from so many different directions that we often take them for granted. Once we take the words for granted, we usually don't notice the moral issues they raise. How should marketers think about the limits of fair advertising? Is it ever legitimate for friends to be manipulative when seeking cooperation? When are white lies okay? The act of thinking about the moral issues raised by everyday speech is itself a demonstration of the power of words and their capacity to change the way we see ourselves and the way we act and interact.

An old Jewish teaching likens the tongue to an arrow. Why not another weapon—a sword, for example? Because, we are told, if a person unsheathes his sword to kill another, the man can be mollified, change his mind and return the sword to its scabbard. However, once an arrow is shot, the archer cannot return it to the bow no matter how much the sender wishes it. Words can inflict devastating and irrevocable harm; therefore, cruel words are compared in the Jewish tradition to weapons that can wound or even kill.   — D.C.S.

The time between ritual handwashing and breaking bread (*motzi*) is supposed to be one of silence. I have observed how hard it is for so many to remain silent even for those few moments. Next time you find yourself in this moment, try not to fear the loss of words or resist the silence. Embrace the silence as passionately as you embrace words, and see what arises in your soul.   — D.J.L.

Jewish tradition has a long history of thinking about the hierarchy of different types of speech and how each should best be employed in the world. Maimonides, in his *Commentary* to *Pirkey Avot,* suggests that all speech falls into five categories: prescribed, including words of Torah; cautioned against, such as slander and gossip; rejected, such as idle talk; desired, such as speech that communicates proper virtue; and permitted, that which is necessary to daily human function.   — N.H.M.

Speech, Autonomy and Community

North Americans live in a world that places an enormous emphasis on individual autonomy. That is particularly the case in the United States. In terms of speech, that means we have the capacity to say or write whatever we wish, whenever we wish and to whomever we wish. In the United States a wide range of obnoxious expression is permitted in the name of free speech and personal autonomy. This is partly about a commitment to personal freedom, but it is no less about the belief that creating an open society is the likeliest way to support democracy, which depends on a free exchange of ideas and information. Most of us highly value that openness even though we might question the good sense or good taste of some of the people who use it without restraint.

It seems to me one impetus toward excessive speech in the 21st century is the extension of a confessional and therapeutic culture which sees psychological flourishing as linked to self-revelation. From Essalen to Oprah the assumption is that exploration of previously private or undisclosed matters is a personal and communal virtue.
— S.F.K.

The emphasis on autonomy often results in people saying whatever they want. By contrast, Jewish tradition has generally placed a greater emphasis on community. Placing less emphasis on self-expression and more on mutuality and cooperation can sometimes feel constraining, and it can have the negative effect of stifling the expression of important and valuable differences. On the other hand, it is clear that unrestrained speech in the form of criticism, gossip, lying or argument can ruin relationships and disrupt a community, making it an unsafe and sometimes painful place to be.

Few would want to legislate undue constraints on speech, although the legal prohibition on hate speech and ethnic derogation in Canada, for example, has some advantages over the greater openness to unlimited speech in the United States. Without legislating speech constraints, we may still wish to take ethical positions that constrain language in ways that support community and avoid unnecessary harm to others.

We should be concerned about what is happening to words in our time and society. Public and private discourse—particularly in the political and religious arenas—has become shrill and potentially dangerous. The airwaves have been flooded by radio "shock jocks" who spew inflammatory language and instigate mistrust. As the ratings thrive, the talk-show hosts are encouraged to raise the decibels of their venom. Careless use of language has heightened the level of heat, anger and hostility in our society. Cruel and thoughtless remarks are bad enough when they are made in private conversation—but when they are amplified through the media and in the realm of entertainment, they begin to acquire an aura of acceptability and credibility. Things become more acceptable when "everybody else is doing it" or "saying it."　— D.C.S.

Safety is a spiritual and ethical issue. Our speech can help create environments that are safe enough to allow the soul to be revealed to ourselves and shared with an other. This is sacred.　— S.P.W.

In a community setting, speech helps to create a common culture, build relationships, teach values, share information, develop a shared vision, divide tasks, negotiate conflict and accomplish many other useful functions. For community to work, speech must be used in ways that are both sufficiently personally expressive and communally productive. The more one cares about emphasizing the infinite worth of each human being (*tzelem Elohim*), sustaining long-term relationships, and supporting a strong community, the more one will seek strong ethical guidance about speech.

According to the Ḥofetz Ḥayim (see *The Third Jewish Catalogue,* p. 94), community may be defined as a group of people who speak to one another about one another. Working within that definition, the content of our speech is a major factor in determining the quality of the communities we inhabit. We can help create the ideal communities we envision by holding ourselves to high standards of discourse.   — D.E.

While placing less emphasis on unrestrained self-expression and more on mutuality and cooperation may lessen discord and argument in community, it can also reduce the truth-telling necessary for communities to grapple with important ethical issues. When individuals break silence and give voice to what has never been spoken in public, ethical awareness can be raised. We saw this when women began to speak out about how domestic violence, sexual harassment and sexual abuse were silently and invisibly destroying the fabric of our communities. We saw this when gay and lesbian Jews began to speak out about the realities of lives lived in silence and were able to bring the fullness of themselves into Jewish community. When we cannot speak openly and safely and share differing views in our communities about Israel, for example, we weaken our communities and the pursuit of justice.   — B.E.B.

Speech is a powerful vehicle for the imagination. The language we use can literally bring worlds together by investing symbols and images with multiple meanings.
— S.P.W.

Jewish tradition teaches that since we are created in the divine image, when we insult or shame another person, we are insulting or shaming God.   — D.C.S.

Jews have long recognized the central importance of community in creating the kind of society they believe in. As a result, Jewish tradition carries strong moral limits on the use of speech. These limits stand in strong tension with contemporary individualism, and finding a balance between them is a central challenge in speech ethics.

Rabbi Ben Zoma asked, "Who is a hero?" and answered: "One who subdues his passion, as it is said, 'One who is slow to anger is better than the mighty who conquer a city.'" (*Pirkey Avot* 4.1) A later commentary adds, "Who is mighty? One who turns his enemy into a friend" (*Avot d'Rabi Natan,* 23). The Jewish moral tradition encourages us to work out our differences with others. "You shall not hate your neighbor in your heart" (Leviticus 19:17). This means that we ought to disclose our feelings and anger in a constructive way to the one with whom we are aggrieved. It means that, as modern counselors would tell us, we ought to focus our anger on the issue and not on the person.   — D.C.S.

In the 1970s, feminist theologian Nelle Morton coined the phrase "hearing into speech" to describe what happened as groups of women came together to share stories of our spiritual journeys, offering "a hearing engaged in by the whole body that evokes speech—a new speech—a new creation." In Jewish feminist communities, women experienced "theologizing as process." Trusting our own experiences of the Holy, we began to transform the language traditionally used for naming and thinking about God. For many women it was the first time we gave primacy to our own experiences of the Holy, rather than ignoring or marginalizing any experiences that did not conform to the received tradition. Jewish tradition granted women no such authority. When we consider the moral limits placed on the use of speech by the tradition, we must always ask: whose speech? Whose authority is being limited? In order for the feminist transformation of Judaism to begin, women needed to form alternative communities in which we could "hear each other into speech." Only when we could speak into the receptive heart of such communities could we find our voices.   — B.E.B.

The tension between individual autonomy and communal consciousness is present in many areas of ethical and religious practice. Once the coercive power of a religious tradition is removed, the choice to accept the imperatives as well as the constraints of the tradition rests with the individual not as an independent agent, but within the context of a community.   — R.H.

Confidentiality, Privacy and the Need to Know

We all have parts of our lives that we would prefer to keep private for legitimate reasons, such as preserving modesty; keeping errors and failings to ourselves; avoiding envy, conflict or competition; saving ourselves or others from embarrassment; or protecting others. In most situations honesty does not require full disclosure—a traumatic mistake made as a child, for example, is rarely relevant to an adult's career or communal roles. Preserving privacy and limiting personal information to those who have a legitimate need to know make sharing community a safer undertaking.

I have always been impressed with the respect for privacy in Jewish tradition from biblical times to the present. "When you make a loan of any sort to your neighbor, you must not enter his house to seize his pledge. You must remain outside, while the man to whom you make the loan brings the pledge out to you" (Deuteronomy 24:10–11). "No one shall open windows facing a jointly owned courtyard.... No one may place an entrance in a courtyard opposite the entrance of another or a window opposite another's window" (*Mishna Bava Batra* 3:7). And, in contemporary times, Section 7 of the Basic Laws of the State of Israel includes: "Every person is entitled to privacy and the confidentiality of information concerning his life." — L.K.

The Jewish tradition has a strong presumption that one should not remind anyone of past failings. Doing so is called *ona'at devarim,* oppression through words. The classic example is reminding a *ger* (convert) of the unsavory religious practices in which the *ger* might have engaged before becoming Jewish. There is a famous talmudic story (*Bava Metzia* 84a) about Resh Lakish, who was a highway bandit and gladiator before doing *teshuva* and becoming a scholar. He was involved in a legal argument as to when a weapon's forging is finished. His colleague, Rabbi Yohanan, jibed, "A robber is an expert in his trade," and further reminded him that it had been Yohanan who brought Resh Lakish back into the fold. The humiliation of this exchange led to Resh Lakish's death. — M.F.

The existence of privacy in a world where information is so plentiful depends on our mutual agreement to respect each other's privacy. Eavesdropping and opening someone else's mail are flagrant examples of violating privacy rights. Of course, the speaker ought to take modest precautions, such as not speaking of private matters in a public place with a loud voice or while talking on a cell phone. Perceiving privacy is a precursor to protecting it.

Jewish law has explicitly protected private correspondence from disclosure for a millennium. Rabbenu Gershom (Germany, late 10th to early 11th centuries) issued a *takana* (legal decree) that prohibited the reading of other peoples' mail, whether for personal gain or mere curiosity. The decree forbade even the reading of mail without disclosing its contents to others and threatened those breaching it with excommunication.   — M.F.

The near-ubiquity of cell phones challenges many of the standards of ethical speech as well as appropriate public behavior. Aside from the rude invasion of public space by loud conversations, the public sharing of the conversation violates the privacy of the person at the other end of the call even if only one side is overheard. People who think they are able to be more efficient by using a cell phone as a "virtual office" too often breach privacy norms. On a recent train ride I—and most of the other passengers—overheard a physician in a loud discussion with his secretary about a patient, whom he named. When I rebuked him, noting that many people had overheard this confidential information, everyone in the car applauded. We have a long way to go before we come to a consensus on a "Torah of the cell phone" that assures privacy and modesty.   — R.H./J.N.

The ease of violating others' privacy through technology can constitute a violation of *lifnei iver lo titen mikhshol*—"Do not place a stumbling-block before the blind." When I sit at the privacy of my desk and search for a high-school classmate on Google, I can find not only contact information but also naïve letters she wrote to the editor of her college newspaper, postings she made to an Internet support group for a rare medical condition, and a complaint about her bed-and-breakfast to the Better Business Bureau. The potential impact on our relationship is clear. The problem is particularly acute in that I may not have intended to find intimate details, but read through sensitive material before realizing it was sensitive. Technology can breach privacy by aggregating information that is legitimately public, but was previously inaccessible on a practical level by reason of obscurity. It is not clear that a legal or technological fix exists for this problem, but a first step is to teach an ethic of self-restraint with regard to seeking out others' personal information. Just because you can learn something doesn't mean that you should.   — M.F.

Sometimes we agree to a partial suspension of privacy, as we do when we give personal information to a physician, rabbi, accountant, therapist or attorney. That person promises to keep our information confidential. This allows us to share information when necessary while still protecting our privacy. A commitment to confidentiality generates a substantial obligation to protect the private information of other people. This obligation can extend to knowledge of what they possess, or what they have done, or what they think. It may involve their characteristics, their relationships or what others think of them.

In the world of email, the use of the "bcc" feature (blind copy) violates privacy when it is used to let a third party or parties see an email that the receiver thinks is a completely private communication. However, in the case of an e-mail sent to a large group, one must use the bcc feature in order to preserve the privacy of the names and addresses in the distribution list. Users of email should not hide behind excuses of "I'm not tech-savvy" to avoid learning how to use the tools of communication because that ignorance has ethical consequences. — S.J.G.

Confidentiality arises out of the interaction between two entities, and is primarily an obligation of the receiving entity not to disclose information tendered to the recipient without permission of the confider. It seems to me that the obligation of confidentiality is largely a question of promise keeping and abiding by voluntarily assumed role constraints: It attaches to the entity that receives and may reveal information. Privacy is a broader concept that protects against involuntary transfer of control over information of a certain sort. Privacy obligations attach not only to a holder of information who obtains it in confidence, but also to anyone tempted to obtain private information and to anyone who obtains information of a private nature innocently (for example, a person who accidentally overhears intimate details on a phone line). Revelation of such information would violate no duties of confidentiality, but could still violate duties to respect privacy. — S.F.K.

Both privacy and confidentiality allow the parties to mark intimacy of relationships: To the extent I share private details of my life only with my friend, doctor, therapist or beloved, I have established a special bond involving mutual recognition and vulnerability. If all information were publicly available, sharing it would have no such impact. — S.F.K.

Confidentiality, however, is not itself an inviolable norm. The commitment to confidentiality is not as great as the commitment to *pikuaḥ nefesh,* saving a life. Similarly some secular law recognizes a psychologist's obligation to warn a third party endangered by the psychologist's patient. Jewish tradition's term for the obligation to warn is *azhara.* The idea that the commitment to confidentiality is not as great as the commitment to preventing serious emotional or physical injury is derived by the rabbis from the dictum *lo ta'amod al dam re'ekha/*do not stand idly by the blood of another person (Leviticus 19:16). This is why the obligation to report physical and sexual abuse takes precedence over confidentiality. The commitment to confidentiality can also be superseded by the need to protect a community. Thus the obligation to protect the privacy of others and promises of confidentiality are not absolute commitments. On the other hand, people holding confidences ought to have powerful reasons if they are considering violating someone else's privacy. Convenience, an opportunity to gossip, the possibility of personal gain or responding to the wishes of others, for example, are not sufficient reasons to violate privacy.

This commandment stands at the center of Torah and in many respects at the pinnacle of Torah teachings.   — T.K.

The requirements for mandated reporting vary from state to state. Synagogues and Jewish agencies should ascertain who on the staff is mandated to report and to whom.   — R.H.

Reporting a wrongdoer to authorities with the power to punish is an obligation that overrides confidentiality when the wrongdoer is likely to continue transgressing in a way that harms others or when the wrongdoing corrodes the community. If the governmental authorities are likely to treat a Jew unfairly or to retaliate against the Jewish community, then turning in a Jew constitutes the crime of being an informer or *malshin*. That venerable historical problem does not exist in modern democracies, so the obligation to turn in wrongdoers has no current constraint of that type in North America, Western Europe or Israel. Secular rules limit reporting; attorneys, for example, do not report the crimes of their clients.

My intuition suggests an obligation in many cases to try to dissuade a friend from further criminal activity, and not to collude in it, but no obligation to report. This is the rule in legal ethics. I am attracted to C.S. Forster's dictum, "If given the choice between betraying my friend and betraying my country, I hope I should have the guts to betray my country" (E.M. Forster, "What I Believe," in *Two Cheers for Democracy* 67, 68 [1951]). — S.F.K.

Some in the Jewish community argue that even if the justice system is not biased against Jews, public exposure of Jews who have acted shamefully gives ammunition to anti-Semites. It is true that there are those who take any instance of wrongdoing by a Jew to be evidence of Jewish iniquity. However, the moral responsibility for such consequences surely lies primarily with the individual Jew and his or her *ḥilul hashem* (diminution of the divine presence). — M.F.

How can we decide when preserving privacy should take precedence and when we should give precedence to other needs? The comparative gains and losses must be weighed. The gains from invading privacy are usually obvious, but some of the largest costs of invading privacy are more subtle. These include not only the short-term strains on relationships and the losses to the person whose privacy has been breached, but the broader erosion of trust, a form of moral and social capital that is critical to sustaining community and building relationships. People's conduct changes when their trust is eroded. They might,

Weighing "comparative gains and losses" of privacy against other needs is no easy matter, made even more difficult by our inability to be objective about ourselves. As it is written (Genesis 2:18): "It is not good for the human to be alone." We need to seek out and to cultivate trusted counsel to help us decide such matters.   — C.H-M.

How do we make these difficult moral judgments? How do we understand our own motivation? How do we get honest with ourselves? Before we speak, we think. What is our relationship with thought? We need to cultivate awareness of what we are thinking and see that we have choices. Ethical guidelines illumine these decision points. Spiritual practices teach us how to look for the moments of choice and identify the patches of delusion, confusion and fear that cloud our vision.   — S.P.W.

Violations of privacy are not always obvious or connected to dramatic issues. Many people have had the uncomfortable experience of hearing a conversation they had with someone replayed to them by a third party.   — R.H.

The suggestion to consider how others will view you if you breach privacy is an important one. A next step could be to actively seek out advice on the matter from a trusted *rav* or friend. *Pirkey Avot* 1.6 says, "Accept a teacher upon yourself; acquire a friend for yourself." We have largely lost the ancient model of apprenticeship in our contemporary culture, and too often, we learn our Torah and our ethics from books and not from actual teachers. "Book ethics" is a beginning, but it is dangerous because we risk making an ideal that has no living human face into an idol.   — J.B.

for example, stop consulting the doctor, therapist or rabbi, or they might become less committed to their employer or friend. Given the high cost of violating privacy, compelling reasons should exist for doing so. One simple way of gaining perspective on a decision involving privacy is to consider how others whose ethics you respect will view you if you breach privacy. Will they find your explanation compelling? Will they appreciate what you have accomplished?

When violating privacy also involves breaching confidentiality, the moral price of doing so increases considerably because such a violation also involves breaking an explicit promise, or at least an implied one, that confidentiality will be maintained. This results in an even more substantial breakdown of trust. Therefore, it is much harder to justify, though the examples above indicate that on very rare occasions, breaching confidentiality may be the right thing to do.

At a workshop I attended dealing with intimate topics, all participants agreed to confidentiality, including among the participants. This meant that no one could raise an issue about me outside a formal group meeting unless I initiated discussion of the issue. No one else had permission to raise my issues with me in an informal setting. I appreciated this privacy guideline.   — S.P.W.

Truth, Lies and Advertising

Rabbinic tradition teaches that the seal of God is *emet,* truth (B. Talmud, *Shabbat* 55a). Seeking truth, attempting to understand our world and thinking about how we ought to act are central preoccupations of Jewish life. One of the ideals for a person is becoming a *dover emet bil'vavo,* one who speaks truth to oneself. Avoiding all forms of deception, including self-deception, is an ideal. As is often the case with ideals, it cannot be fully attained in our flawed world without unacceptable consequences. Deciding how much truth to tell is an ongoing challenge.

Within Jewish tradition two approaches developed around truth telling. One says that saying anything less than the whole, unvarnished truth is inadequate. Rabbis from the early sage Shammai through Rambam of medieval Egypt (see *Mada, Hilkhot De'ot* 2.6) have reflected this idealistic perspective. However, most of our tradition's sources reflect a concern that this is a rigid and potentially painful way to live, both for the speaker and the receivers. Hillel, for example, proclaims that everyone should be able to tell a bride that she is beautiful on her wedding day. (*Ketubot* 16b-17a) While clearly an affectively appropriate remark, it is not always an accurate description. Shammai disagrees with Hillel, but traditional practice follows Hillel. The per-

There may be unacceptable consequences to avoiding all forms of deception, but avoiding all forms of self-deception does not carry such consequences. Seeking to be honest with ourselves is an important tool for self-improvement. The greater our ability to live without delusions, the greater the likelihood is that others will speak to us truthfully. The absence of self-deception helps us bring out the best in ourselves and in others.   — D.E.

spective reflected in this approach recognizes that while pursuing truth is of high importance, speech has other vital functions as well. Helping a bride to feel beautiful on her wedding day has long been one of them.

Telling an unattractive bride that she is beautiful is a "white lie" that almost anyone would condone because it is not a statement meant to convey a literal truth, but rather to add to the joy and meaning of her wedding day. In our time, we would say that the same holds true for a groom. On the other hand, a salesman trying to unload a particularly hard-to-sell and ill-fitting suit might say to a customer that it is a highly desirable garment that makes him look handsome.

Hillel is really saying that there is no such thing as a bride who is not lovely. Even if we see her as unattractive, to say that she is beautiful is not so much a lie as it is a correction to our superficial and damaging tendency to categorize and judge women as "pretty" or "ugly." The truth is that in her role as the joyful and chosen bride, she is indeed beautiful and lovely. Through language that speaks a deeper truth, we actually instruct ourselves to see things that we may be culturally programmed to overlook. Through our habits of speech, we can actually train ourselves to think and see differently.   — V.M.

I worry about the use of the phrase, "white lie." Leaving aside issues of racial sensitivity and privileging, it seems to me far too vague and tempting an escape from ethical obligation. Even if necessary in pursuit of other supervening goals, the lie should still be acknowledged as such. A contrary approach makes it all too easy to categorize convenient untruths as white lies. It seems to me that the appropriate approach is to find ways to convey the "affective truth" without telling a lie (e.g., "You look radiant"). The effort may uncover real compliments that can be given without straining the truth. Even if well-motivated and harmless to others, outright falsehoods corrode the habits of character that underwrite ethical behavior.   — S.F.K.

In *Tales of Love and Darkness* (p. 112), Amos Oz speaks about his grandfather. "He was always attracted to women—all women, both the beautiful ones and those whose beauty other men were incapable of seeing. 'Women,' my grandfather once declared, 'are all very beautiful. All of them without exception. Only men,' he smiled, 'are blind! *Nu,* what. They only see themselves, and not even themselves. Blind!'"   — S.P.W.

This could result in the customer buying the suit, wasting his money and perhaps wearing a garment that makes him look bad. Such a lie is wrong because it is a form of *g'nevat da'at,* theft by deceit, as is misrepresenting credentials or accomplishments. These actions not only constitute the serious crime of theft; they also involve the damage that comes from misleading, from planting a lie in someone's mind.

Another form of lying is claiming the work of others as one's own. This, too, is a form of *g'nevat da'at,* for it induces people to believe that something is the speaker or writer's creation when it is not. This lie is often achieved by silence. In not giving credit, one creates the illusion that the work is one's own. The Jewish principle is that the inventor of an idea or phrase should always receive credit for it, that it should be cited *b'shem omro,* in the name of

Failing to attribute sources even once can permanently damage the speaker's reputation for integrity. If congregants learn that the rabbi's sermon presented as her own was in fact taken off the Internet, they will rightly wonder what else the rabbi may have misrepresented.   — R.H.

When we speak *b'shem omro,* rather than appearing unoriginal, we are acknowledging that we are part of a larger conversation. When we realize that the goal is not necessarily to have a *ḥidush,* a new insight, of one's own, but to collectively create and engage, it changes not only *what* we say, but the very way we speak. So many of our speaking tendencies are patterned around self-preservation and self-promotion. Crediting others reminds us that we are part of a larger web.   — J.B.

The compound transgression of stealing someone else's work and misrepresenting oneself as the author is abetted by the Internet. With the widespread availability of research papers online has come a dramatic increase in plagiarism. More troubling, college professors increasingly report that students who are caught often do not understand that they have committed a violation.   — R.H.

While intellectual honesty is important, the contemporary American legal landscape goes substantially beyond the insistence that others' ideas be credited. Some-the one who first spoke it. Theft of credit through silence is no less a form of theft.

When is it all right to lie? The Rambam's solution to this problem is that the only alternative to telling the truth is silence, but many people would agree that some white lies are acceptable. One test is whether, if the lie were disclosed, people with good moral judgment would say that they would tell such a lie themselves. Other questions worth asking are whether the purpose of the lie is to benefit the recipient rather than the speaker, and whether believing the lie could in any way damage the hearer or others. It might also be helpful to ask about the impact of the lie on the community. Compliments, avoidance of embarrassment, and encouragement might, under some circumstances, involve white lies. A speaker who lies for personal gain, or to conceal his/her incompetence or failure to perform, or to protect a guilty party, for example, is guilty not only of lying but of *g'nevat da'at.*

times copyright restrictions don't expire until several decades after an author dies. Jewish scholarship over the generations has flourished precisely because of the dual ethic of free-ranging discussion of other's viewpoints while carefully crediting their origin. The zeal of large media companies to protect their profits may have tipped the balance too far away from the open exchange of cultural and intellectual expression that is central to civilization's progress. — M.F.

Pikuaḥ nefesh/saving a life is a legitimate reason not to tell the truth. We praise Shifra and Puah, the Egyptian midwives in Exodus who refused Pharaoh's order to kill the Jewish infant boys, claiming that the Jewish women delivered their children too quickly. We honor people like Raoul Wallenberg and Varian Fry, who issued false documents to Jews in order to save them during the Holocaust. And ordinary Americans of that period who signed untrue documents claiming Jews in Europe as relatives, perhaps because of a similar last name, were performing honorable deeds in trying to save them. — R.P.T.

These criteria have important applications in regard to considering the issue of propriety of advertising. Some degree of exaggeration is so expected that it is not taken seriously: "Discriminating people say that this is the best peanut butter in the world!" Such matters of opinion are not heard as literal truth. Other statements are made in a way that creates an expectation that they are literally true: "This truck gets 27 miles per gallon on the highway." Falsifying such a statement is *g'nevat da'at.*

More complicated are advertisements that manipulate feelings, creating a desire for an unneeded product or encouraging people to select products for reasons not intrinsic to the product. Advertising that manipulates in order to create a market for a product is destructive to the truth, as well as to trust in commercial dealings. On the other hand, advertising that helps people find merchan-

Although we are used to hearing and discounting exaggerated language claiming salvific effects for various products, such use of language is damaging. It creates false expectations and makes us less likely to believe in other, more promising paths to improving our world. — D.E.

Midrash Hagadol (Yemen, 12th century) says that purchasing someone's field by trading a donkey that you know is in bad health is a violation of *lifney iver* (putting a stumbling block before the blind, Leviticus 19:14) since the other person is "blind" to the true circumstances. We can surely think of contemporary parallels to the donkey's concealed defect. — R.P.T.

The issue of advertising that creates a market for an unnecessary product by manipulating consumers cannot be separated from the larger economic and political context. It is not only extravagant and unnecessary material products that are foisted on the public. Too many public leaders create a "market" for a program or proposal, and even for military action, by manipulating messages and misrepresenting information. — R.H.

dise at a fair price or creates awareness for better products
is filling a useful purpose.

Limiting Speech, Avoiding Gossip, Giving References

The limitations placed on speech in order to preserve truth
and protect privacy and confidentiality are far from the
only ones. Saying more than is necessary can often do
harm. Speaking in anger often generates more heat than
light. Waiting to calm down, speaking in "I" statements,
avoiding insults and the restatement of old hurts, and
looking for common ground before exploring areas of
conflict can all be valuable in sparing feelings and healing
relationships.

The Jacob and Esau story provides a biblical metaphor for manipulative advertising.
Jacob is the arch deceiver, pretending to be someone and something he is not in
order to fulfill his desire for blessing—power, privilege, wealth. We need to cultivate and strengthen the perception of Isaac inside ourselves when he says, "The
voice is the voice of Jacob, yet the hands are the hands of Esau" (Genesis 27:22). We
must separate the clever and appealing message from the frivolous or unwholesome
product.   — S.P.W.

Giving advice to another person is a serious responsibility when you have knowledge that the other person lacks. Misleading or false advice is especially wrong. The
rabbis say, "'Putting a stumbling block before the blind': What does this mean?
Before one who is blind to the matter. If someone asks your advice, do not give inappropriate advice. Don't say, 'Leave early in the morning' when you know robbers
will be waiting for him. Don't say, 'Leave at noon' if you know that hot sun will
harm her" (*Sifre* on Leviticus 19:14, paraphrased).   — R.P.T.

People with good sense are careful when people ask them what they think of others. Hurt feelings, damaged relationships and other repercussions can come from their answers. The most obvious problem with gossip is that it always has a person that it treats as the object of the gossip. Jewish tradition teaches that every human being is made *b'tzelem Elohim,* in the image of God, so each person should be treated with deep respect as a reflection of the Source of all worth. The use of words should add to the meaning and value in our lives, not demean them. "God says of one who speaks *l'shon hara* (bad speech), 'We cannot dwell together in the world'" (Talmud, *Arakhin* 15a).

The proper dispensation of praise for praiseworthy acts or character is both a moral good and a communal virtue. *Hakarat hatov,* recognizing the good—good deeds, good character, good judgment and courageous action—deserves our attention. That recognition can shape both character and culture. — S.F.K.

Some sociologists and anthropologists argue that gossip is a morally valuable way to establish and maintain community norms and to exercise the faculties of moral judgment. If we forgo negative gossip, we will need other means to accomplish these ends. One strategy that can help is following the rabbinic dictum, *dan l'khaf z'khut,* judge favorably (see *Pirkey Avot* 1.6). Positive statements about others can portray moral models. When members of a community see others favorably, circulation of information is less likely to be corrosive of community. — S.F.K.

While we are now careful to be gender-neutral when talking about gossip, the legacy of the *yenta* stereotype is strong. Jewish tradition had a long history of condemning or circumscribing women's speech. Yosi Ben Yoḥanan warns in *Pirkey Avot* (1:5) "Do not talk too much with women, even one's wife—how much more to another man's wife." This led the sages to say, "One who talks too much with a woman brings disaster upon himself, begins to neglect Torah, and ends up an heir to Gehenna." These types of injunctions have historically denigrated women's speech as less valuable than the speech of men in religious and business realms. Although we know that injunctions against *l'shon hara* are equally applicable to women and men, we need to keep in mind that we are still working against the stereotype of the Jewish woman who can't control her tongue, nags about inconsequential things and, at her worst, can lure men away from Torah and into suffering with her speech. — N.H.M.

Gossip that involves repeating unflattering facts has the capacity to do irreparable harm to the individuals discussed. Exchanging information about our lives, building relationships, and networking are not forms of gossip, though they are sometimes unfairly and incorrectly categorized that way. Gossip involves statements that are damaging. When those damaging statements are true, they are usually known as *l'shon hara,* bad speech, following the usage in the definitive 19th century treatise *Ḥofetz Ḥayim.* Such gossiping need not be done with ill intent in order to be damaging. The original speaker cannot know its effect on the hearer or on anyone else who hears it later. A person who listens to *l'shon hara* without a morally significant reason to do so is a partner in an immoral act. After all, gossip requires both a speaker and a listener. The preferable response is asking the speaker to stop or simply walking away.

Gossip violates the prohibition on cursing or insulting the deaf (Leviticus 19:14). "One who curses his friend [who is not present] violates the commandment that says 'You shall not curse the deaf'" (B. Talmud, *Shevuot* 36a). It is just as wrong to speak negatively of an absent person who cannot hear your words as it is to speak negatively about a deaf person who is present. — R.P.T.

During a divorce, it is particularly important to avoid saying negative things to one's children about the other parent, no matter how angry one is. It is never good for children to hate or be estranged from their parent(s). — J.N.

The temptation to share information about a third party is often motivated by a desire to establish or deepen one's rapport with the person with whom you are sharing the information. Thus, it often *feels* as if it's the right thing to do—because it seems as if it is demonstrating your trust in the other person. It is a good example of the rabbis' description of the *yetzer hara* (evil inclination) as evil that masquerades as good. In fact, if you break the confidence of a third party with me, I am *less* likely to trust you with my own vulnerability. — J.J.S.

The Talmud (*Ketubot* 5b) teaches that our earlobes are soft and flexible for the purpose of using them to plug our ears when we need to stop ourselves from listening. — V.M.

One image from Jewish tradition about this kind of gossip is that it is like the feathers from a pillow getting loose outdoors—it is almost impossible to undo. *L'shon hara* has other negative effects as well. It undermines trust because anyone who hears it knows that people could just as easily spread *l'shon hara* about them. Every time one hears *l'shon hara,* one is more likely to speak *l'shon hara* because gossip can become culturally accepted behavior, as newspaper gossip columns and many popular magazines demonstrate. Gossip can be understood as a form of individual expression, as it usually is in North America, but Jewish ethics demands that it be understood primarily as a behavior that is destructive to relationships and to community.

At least a pillow contains a finite number of feathers. An email, on the other hand, can be forwarded *ad infinitum.* — M.F.

Relating private conversations or personal interactions to someone who cannot know the full context should also be considered *l'shon hara.* One all-too-common example is the congregational meeting convened to discuss extending the rabbi's contract. This is a bad practice on many levels, but especially because any grievance aired in such a public forum must be considered *l'shon hara.* With perhaps the best of intentions, the congregation's leaders create a situation in which gossip is all but unavoidable. — C.H-M.

Not only is gossip culturally accepted behavior, it is an economic engine that drives pulp publications and celebrity-focused television shows. Gossip sells as it corrupts civility. — R.H.

Contrasting with traditional teachings against gossip, some feminist writers see "gossip" as an important mode of learning about human relationships. Women in particular have used conversations about their relationships and families as part of a networking process. — R.P.T.

But not all forms of *l'shon hara* are to be shunned. If someone in the process of hiring a bookkeeper asks another employer about a former employee who embezzled money, the former employer has an obligation to warn in order to avoid leaving a stumbling block before the blind (*mikhshol lifney iver*). This is *l'shon hara* that ought to be done for a morally compelling reason. In such cases, I need to weigh whether telling or withholding will do the greater harm. Of course, I should never speak ill of anyone unless I have firsthand information about the facts. If the embezzler worked not for me but someone else, it would be more correct to say, "I believe that it is very important that you find out about the candidate from former employers, since I believe they could have some important things to tell you, and I have only a personal relationship. . . ."

In contemporary American culture, the pledge to hold information in confidence is a very serious and powerful one that feels inviolable. "I promised to keep the information confidential, so my hands are tied!" Thus, it is extremely important to consider the competing values. If someone has shared with me a concern about his/her own problematic behavior, *and* I know that s/he has subsequently repeated the pattern and hurt others *and* has not sought help, I am obliged to disclose what needs to be disclosed to others who have been hurt or who are likely to be hurt. To do less is to become complicit.   — J.J.S.

Rabbi Israel Salanter, a 19th-century moralist, differentiates between varying degrees of *l'shon hara*. For example, "If you were to say of your rabbi that he does not have a good voice and of your cantor that he is not a scholar—you are a gossip. But if you were to say of your rabbi that he is no scholar and of a cantor that he has no voice—you are a murderer."   — D.C.S.

If someone asks for a reference regarding a third person, to avoid *l'shon hara* and bad feelings it is wise to speak only with that person's explicit permission and then only with great care. The task in that case is to provide useful and honest information while doing as little *l'shon hara* as possible. For example, "Jane was very reliable as a receptionist, she learned routines quickly, and she always worked diligently." This does not reveal that she was never promoted because she did not work independently, but it does provide an accurate description of what she was good at, which is probably helpful both to Jane and the potential employer. Whenever possible, we should limit statements to giving facts ("He embezzled $11,000 in 2004") rather than opinions or judgments ("He is a thief"). As a reference, I want to serve the interests of all concerned, and a carefully done reference can do that.

Revealing only information that reflects positively on the applicant when providing a reference to a potential employer is potentially misleading unless the interlocutor is familiar with your procedure. The prospective employer may rely to her detriment on an assumption that your speech has fully disclosed concerns about the prospective employee. On the other hand, if the prospective employer knows the game, the comment that "Jane is reliable as a receptionist" effectively conveys the further information that Jane had other defects. If so, you may not have avoided *l'shon hara*.   — S.F.K.

Many companies today are concerned about the legal ramifications of giving a negative reference for a former employee. Policies are carefully drawn up by legal teams that limit what can and cannot be said about a person's tenure. These sometimes are limited to confirming employment dates and position.   — N.H.M.

Of course, not all information that could be shared involves *l'shon hara*. If I tell mutual friends of someone's illness so that they will visit (*bikur ḥolim*), bring food or at least send a card, that is a wonderful thing to do. On the other hand, the ill person may consider it an invasion of privacy if someone gives intimate details about the nature of the illness to those who have no need to know, or even spreads word of the illness to those who will not come forward to help. Invasion of privacy is problematic by itself, and it often leads to *l'shon hara*. "You're telling me Jon missed more work because he was sick again? I don't see how he keeps his job." "Being married to Jon is certainly no picnic." "Jon's illnesses drain a lot of the community's resources."

We live in societies that frequently require evaluations of others. Teachers grade students; supervisors evaluate staff; and sometimes staff evaluate peers or supervisors. In some organizations, employees are asked to write annual self-evaluations. How much self-criticism is required? Reporting that we are perfect in every way is wrong, but we don't need to volunteer every failing. At times we need to evaluate candidates for positions at work or as volunteers. These discussions involve consideration of the skills and experience of the candidates. No one is equally talented at everything. How can we conduct such discussions ethically? I suggest limiting the size of the decision-making group, focusing on the relative strengths of candidates, treating areas of weakness gently, and avoiding unnecessary personal comments. Attempts to attack candidates on a personal basis are clearly unethical. Arguing about candidates' proposed policies and their abilities to carry them out is a legitimate function.   — R.P.T.

When sharing with the intention of exploring something about myself, I share information about a parent, sibling or close friend. In such a case, provided the information is shared with discretion and respect, I do not think it constitutes *l'shon hara*.   — D.J.L.

Synagogues often add the names of ill congregants to the public list of those included in prayers for healing without first asking permission of the ill person or that person's family. This reveals private information that some people do not want to be public knowledge.   — R.H.

The safest way to deal with issues about personal information that someone might prefer to keep private is to ask for guidance from that person. Explaining what one would like to do with the information will generally elicit a clear response. A person who is ill or the ill person's family, who may be otherwise in need of support, may prefer to avoid the loss of privacy involved. Such issues should be negotiated gently because people should be able to limit access to private information about themselves.

What kind of information is legitimately public? Matters of public record include such things as births (and therefore

When sharing confidences, a reciprocal responsibility is in force. The listener must be aware of the responsibility not to listen to gossip and not to repeat what is told even if it is not in the category of *l'shon hara*. Similarly, the speaker must be careful not to violate any confidences or put the listener in an uncomfortable position. Both must be clear about their expectations of the conversation. — N.H.M.

A person's sexual orientation and gender identity should always be treated as "personal information." This is not always obvious to everyone and thus bears emphasis. People may infer that because someone has come out as gay or lesbian in a particular community, this means that it is public information. Coming out, as the saying goes, is a process rather than an event—often a lifelong process. Given the fact that our society is hetero-normative, people assume that I am straight unless told otherwise, and I thus have to choose when and where to come out as gay. Someone may be completely out in one community and not be out at work or in another community. In addition, it may be important to me to come out to a particular person rather than having him or her find out from you—even if it's not a secret. In general, therefore, it is safest not to "out" another. — J.J.S.

While a person's coupled or single status may be a matter of public record, the traditional Jewish enterprise of matchmaking is nevertheless complicated. Matchmaking assumes that everyone wants to be coupled and welcomes unsolicited assistance. In fact, some singles choose to remain single. Others feel discomfort at the prospect of being talked about and assessed for the likelihood that they might be "right" for another. Still others have no such discomfort and welcome any and all *shidukhim* (matches). Thus, no matter how much one is motivated by a desire to be helpful, it is important to ask directly whether your help is wanted. — J.J.S.

the names of children or grandchildren), deaths, places of employment, volunteer offices held, books published, weddings (and therefore marital status) and, in increasing numbers of places, same-sex commitment ceremonies. Beyond these basic facts, things become more complicated. Most people keep private many of the personal facts legitimately reported about such public figures as politicians running for major offices. Personal information that one person chooses to place in the public domain may be considered entirely private by someone else. When in doubt, it is better to err on the side of avoiding possible *l'shon hara*.

Jewish tradition teaches that comments heard in a group of more than three people can be assumed to be widely known. If we believe it is appropriate to share a confidence, we should be cautious about doing so with more than one person at a time.
— D.E.

It is helpful to differentiate between privacy, secrecy and intimacy. With regard to certain matters, there ought to be a presumption of privacy. A reasonable (though imperfect) yardstick is whether we would want similar information about ourselves shared without our permission. With regard to other matters, we can assume secrecy, even if we are not explicitly told so, by assessing the impact of disclosure. The category of intimacy is perhaps the most difficult to decode. Intimacy is a function of a relationship between people who know and trust each other enough to share things they would not share (or want shared) with many other people. We can identify issues of intimacy as those that, if shared, would harm or end the relationship. Sharing intimate information outside of the relationship where it lives is a transgression of trust. — R.H.

Sometimes people talk about third parties because they are trying to figure out what is going on with them, or how to help them, or what has happened between them. Making it possible to provide help opens the way to doing *mitzvot,* so it has considerable value. Resolving differences and tensions is a critical part of sustaining relationships, so conversations with that intent have a legitimate place. The challenge regarding such conversations is to avoid providing data for future *l'shon hara.* If the purpose of the conversation is only to exchange information, issues of privacy and *l'shon hara* probably override the potential gains.

Can the person whose advice is being sought be trusted to keep the conversation confidential? The likelihood of that can be ascertained in part by previous personal experience. Even if there is a high likelihood based on past experience, people generally keep confidentiality only if explicitly asked to do so. The time to ask is before the con-

By talking with others about the behavior of third parties, we learn how to understand people, including ourselves. We do this routinely when we study literature, including biblical and other Jewish literature, but when we engage in such discussions about people we know, we typically violate traditional Jewish teachings surrounding *l'shon hara.* The benefits of such discussions need to be carefully weighed against the harm they can cause.   — D.E.

For me, the challenge regarding conversations about third parties is not only to avoid providing data for future *l'shon hara,* but to avoid slipping out of "helping" mode and into "annoyed" mode. In reviewing information regarding students or congregants, I sometimes get exasperated and roll my eyes when I hear that someone is yet again in need of an intervention. I try to remind myself and those with whom I work that we are speaking about the person as allies engaged in an act of love, and not as accomplices committing *l'shon hara.*   — V.M.

versation begins so that the person can decline to have the conversation if keeping it confidential imposes too much of a burden. That burden might be in the form of a possible conflict of interest or simply because of the temptation to gossip. In deciding whether to have a conversation about a third party, its potential initiator should consider whether the potential conversation's likely positive results outweigh the possible dangers. Care in such matters helps community members to maintain control of the private information about themselves.

What do we do when someone has hurt or angered us and we need to talk about it with a third party in order to process the experience? Seeking help that leads to a dissipation of pain and thus a healing of the relationship may sometimes be interpreted as "for the greater good," but sometimes it's just personal. The traditional restrictions here seem to direct us to maintain silence and to repress our feelings in an unhealthy way. In such cases, I seek a confidant whom I know to be trustworthy. When possible, I try to tell my story in a way that masks the identity of the person I am talking about. And I try to tell the story in a way that makes it as clear as I can that my reactions are my intended focus and not the actions that prompted my reactions. In the end, however, the principle that I should never report on the behavior of another in a way that reflects negatively on him or her is not one that I can follow absolutely.   — J.J.S.

Many single people meet other people, including potential spouses or partners, through introductions or recommendations from friends. Clearly there is room for promoting connections in a positive way. Yet at times we may have negative information about someone. Our sources recognized that there were times when encouraging a relationship with major pitfalls was unethical. For example, telling a *kohen* (priest) that a particular woman would be a great match when you know he is not eligible to marry her is considered a violation of *lifnei iver,* putting a stumbling block before the blind. (*Midrash Hagadol* on Leviticus 19). Reconstructionists do not continue the traditions of a *kohen* being forbidden to marry a convert or divorcee. However, we have an obligation to prevent potential harm or deception in relationships if we have definite knowledge.   — R.P.T.

Slander and Malicious Speech

While *l'shon hara* is morally wrong unless it serves a greater good, its moral error pales beside that of gossip that is intended to harm and gossip containing falsehoods. The Rambam and Ḥofetz Ḥayim refer to gossip with the intent to harm as *rekhilut,* and to false statements about others as *motzi shem ra,* creating a bad reputation.

No justification for any kind of *rekhilut* or *motzi shem ra* has ever been offered. Furthering ill will and lying are both moral wrongs. When they have the result of unfairly injuring the reputation of someone or generating bad feeling between people, they are serious moral violations. *Pirkei Avot* 4.17 describes maintaining a *keter shem tov,* a

---

The meaning of *rakhil* in the Bible is uncertain. The word probably derives from merchants who were in a unique position to spread information from community to community. — T.K.

Rav Yoḥanan, in the name of Rav Shammai ben Yoḥai, teaches that verbal *ona'a* (oppression) is a greater sin than monetary *ona'a,* since monetary damages can be corrected through compensation, but damages incurred by inappropriate speech cannot (B. Talmud *Baba Metzia* 58b). — N.H.M.

A powerful example of the life-threatening aspect of *rekhilut* is found in 1 Kings 21, where Queen Jezebel arranges for two individuals to make false claims against Naboth, resulting in his wrongful death by stoning. The wrongs done through *rekhilut* impact on the murdered individual and his family, and also reflect on the extreme corruption in the monarchy. — T.K.

To some, the prohibition against engaging in *rekhilut* extends to never speaking about third parties when they are not present even if one is honestly complimenting or speaking highly of them. While this could seem extreme, not to mention impractical, it nevertheless reminds us of the challenge to be wholly present with the person with whom we are talking. Rather than talking together about a third party's foibles or good points, the task is to really turn to one another and meet. — J.B.

spotless reputation, as the highest of achievements. Damaging someone's reputation without sufficient justification is stealing something of considerable value. Often the damage cannot be fully repaired once it has been done. Thus *rekhilut* and *motzi shem ra* are very serious matters. Feeling angry, envious or jealous does not justify committing such acts, nor does a desire for revenge or for damage to the reputation of an arrogant or overly competitive person.

Casting aspersions on an ethnic, racial or religious group or on an organization or social group is also a form of *rekhilut*. Of course sometimes there is a duty to warn *(azhara),* as is the case, for example, with cults and groups that aim to convert Jews, or those that deceive or waste resources. But speaking negatively when there is no major reason to do so is not only *rekhilut;* it can also give rise to *sinat ḥinam,* baseless hatred, which Jewish tradition suggests is the sin for which the Temple was destroyed.

The psalmist had a profound understanding of the pain that slander could cause an individual and the community. In the psalms of lament, the petitioning sufferer would often claim that his enemies were speaking falsehood against him and that his world was crumbling because of these lies. God is upheld as one who fights against lies and false words, as in Psalm 5, where God is described as dooming those who speak lies.   — T.K.

Divorce is a common situation hospitable to *rekhilut*. One side often has a great need to speak badly about the ex-partner. Speaking this way is a source of relief and self-justification, and it may be part of the healing process and of breaking one's isolation. Sometimes it is hard to talk about anything else. Yet it can also indulge self-pity and reinforce victimhood and resentment, which are immobilizing. It is challenging to be a supportive friend and not play into this pattern.   — S.P.W.

Gossip does not give the people being spoken about an opportunity to defend themselves, or at least to share their perspective or side of the story. The notion of "innocent until proven guilty" should apply here.   — D.J.L.

Many people engage in *motzi shem ra* without consciously doing so because they have heard gossip and repeated it without realizing that it is not true. When it comes to gossip, there is no such thing as a sufficiently reliable witness. One reason to avoid doing *l'shon hara* is that it often contains at least a small amount of unintentional falsehood because details and stories change with each telling. False statements do not have to reach the legal level of libel for them to be heavily damaging and morally reprehensible. Families and communities have an obligation to teach children to avoid *l'shon hara* and *rekhilut*.

A community that experiences *rekhilut* with any frequency often finds that it drives out good and caring people and leaves those who take pleasure in back-biting.

False testimony was an area of great concern for our ancestors. Deuteronomy 19 goes so far as to prescribe that "If the man who testified is a false witness, if he has testified falsely against his fellow, you shall do to him as he schemed to do to his fellow." Israel's neighbors shared the same concern. The Mesopotamian Code of Hammurabi begins with a series of laws against false accusation. If one's word could not be trusted, then the very foundations of law and order were threatened.   — T.K.

Synagogues and rabbinical associations are among the many organizations that provide Internet listserv discussion sites for members. The tendency for postings to orbit around topics that could reasonably fall into the category of *l'shon hara* if not *rekhilut* (although *rekhilut* certainly puts in its appearance) is a cause for concern. Until we arrive at a "Torah of the Internet" that gives ethical guidance about this still relatively new form of communication, we would do well to consider what we would say if we were in a room with the same people instead of online. If we could learn to take that step before hitting the "send" button, a lot of unnecessary and hurtful communication would not occur.   — R.H.

Even when good people don't leave, they often retreat into inactivity and lowered commitment. That leaves the community at the mercy of those who are not bothered by *rekhilut*. Establishing and teaching norms designed to combat *motzi shem ra, rekhilut* and *l'shon hara* is important for the community's long-term welfare. If the community is committed to upholding Jewish values, undertaking this cultural change is a matter of considerable spiritual significance. Making these changes may be a source of short-term conflict in a community, but this is a conflict undertaken *l'shem Shamayim,* for the sake of pursuing an ultimate good.

In order for a community to succeed in such cultural change, it is useful for people to identify the desire and enjoyment element in *rekhilut.* It is hard to give up something without admitting that it has a lot to offer. Then one needs to identify the actual and potential pain and harm caused in order to make it worth foregoing the pleasure. The tool of awareness is critical to this process of *t'shuva* on both an individual and a communal level.   — S.P.W.

Rigorous and sustained personal example is one of the best ways to create cultural change around issues of speech.   — D.E.

Offering Reproof

Providing moral guidance is a responsibility of parents, teachers, supervisors and coaches, among others. Jewish tradition goes further, teaching that it is a responsibility incumbent upon each of us whenever we see someone doing wrong who might stop if we spoke up. *Hokheaḥ tokhi'aḥ,* proclaims Leviticus 19:17, "You shall surely reprove."

The basis of human society is trust that people will conduct themselves in a manner that allows us to be safe in their company. When there is a threat to a community's moral life, each person has an obligation to address that threat. When people do bad things without receiving a critique, they assume that their conduct is being accepted, and when others see a wrongdoer, they assume they are observing proper conduct. Doing *tokheha,* offering reproof, not only has a potential positive effect on the conduct of the

---

The obligation to reprove should be paired with the obligation to judge favorably (*Pirkey Avot* 1.6). Self-righteousness is an appealing posture, and emerging evidence suggests that engaging in "altruistic punishment" triggers some of the same neurological brain rewards as cocaine. (See De Quervain, et al. "The Neural Basis of Altruistic Punishment," *Science,* August 2004.) Offering reproof is too likely to be great fun, and possibly addictive, to be invoked without substantial constraint.   — S.F.K.

How important and challenging offering reproof is, particularly in the context of close personal relationships. Not only is it critical to be able to offer criticisms sensitively and carefully, but it is also important to be able to receive such words without immediately responding defensively and with counterattacks.   — D.J.L.

Having a legitimate critique to offer does not by itself justify doing *tokheha.* We must assess the ability of the person to benefit from the critique prior to offering it. Most people are able to benefit from insight that allows them to take one small step forward. Frequently asking for more change than that makes it difficult for people to take advantage of even a lovingly delivered critique.   — D.E.

person reproved; it also reminds the person offering the reproof not to emulate bad conduct. In the long run, it can have an important impact on the community as a whole by providing a counter-example to the initial impropriety.

The method of offering reproof is critical to its success. Done badly, it can create defensiveness, resistance and defiance. Gentleness, clarity and avoidance of hostility are important. Speaking in a way that recognizes and reaffirms the person's essential goodness and expressing genuine caring for the person help to make *tokheḥa* successful.

The Jewish moral tradition calls upon us to reprove or rebuke others for their wrong actions. There are times when it is appropriate, in fact obligatory, to rebuke our neighbor, our loved one. However, we are reminded that we are not to do so by shaming the person to the point where he turns white from shame (". . . his blood spills within him" B. Talmud, *Arakhin* 16b). The rabbis labored to develop appropriate means to deliver public rebuke and were cautious and humble enough to express doubt as to whether there existed a person who knew how to properly give or accept rebuke.   — D.C.S.

As a matter of practical human relations, gentleness and caring should be accompanied by reminding wrongdoers of their own ideals. Calling someone to account for behavior in terms of community norms is not as effective as reminding people that they want to live admirable lives. S.F.K.

Tokheḥa (reproof) sounds so self-righteous to me. My teacher Sylvia Boorstein states that it is always correct to assume that we each are doing the best that we can. If I could have done better, I would have. This practice works for me in helping me to temper reproof with compassion. In one way or another, I want to say, "I'm sure you didn't mean it, but. . . ."   — J.J.S.

Jewish tradition is sensitive to the difficulties of both offering and receiving reproof. One of the ways we can create a climate that permits reproof is by learning to accept criticism well. The benefit of justified reproof belongs to the one doing the receiving rather than the delivering. If we encourage others to come to us with critique, we are more likely to receive it.   — D.E.

Most people want to do the right thing and act in a way that their peers approve of. That is why a gentle and caring reproof is so often successful.

In rare instances, previous experience with wrongdoers makes it clear that they are unwilling to change. If *tokheḥa* will not succeed, then Jewish tradition says not to offer it, lest doing so cause more harm than good. (See Rambam, *Mishneh Torah, Mada*, Ethics, 6.6–8.) Such harm could involve damaging relationships, or causing humiliation, or increasing the person's determination to act wrongly, or any combination of these things. In situa-

These issues are just as important in the workplace as in the home or synagogue. In offering *tokheḥa,* we do well to keep three principles in mind: Avoid criticizing the person, but rather comment on the behavior; do not presume to know what another person is thinking or feeling; and act promptly after the offending event. For example: YOU: Do you have a few minutes? There's something I'd like to ask you about. OTHER: Sure. What's up? YOU: I was disturbed by something that happened in yesterday's meeting. I was very uncomfortable with the way Plony's ideas (Plony is the Talmud's John Doe) were received. OTHER: What do you mean? YOU: Well, if I had been Plony, I would have been embarrassed by the way people responded. I would have felt attacked for offering unusual suggestions. So I'm not surprised that Plony didn't say anything for the rest of that meeting. OTHER: Are you saying I attacked Plony? YOU: No. What I'm saying is that our behavior might have embarrassed Plony publicly. So I apologized privately to Plony afterward and will apologize publicly at our next group meeting. I'd encourage you to do the same because I'd hate to think that Plony might consider you to be an unkind person.   — C.H-M.

Leviticus 19:18 states: "Hate not your brother in your heart, reprove your counterpart and bear not a sin on his account." The connection between the first phrase, "hate not . . ." and the rest of the verse is that if you start off with hatred in your heart, you will not be able to reprove. You must first turn your heart to a loving position so that you will be able to reprove successfully.   — V.M.

tions where offering *tokheḥa* is not a sensible choice, avoiding any association with the wrongdoing is the next best alternative. If offering reproof to a stranger might result in a violent response, no *tokheḥa* should be offered.

It is critical for the person offering reproof to be certain that he understands all the dimensions of the perceived wrong. I know of a woman who brought her husband to the Wall in Jerusalem and, even though he suffered from the early stages of Alzheimer's disease, stood by as he went up to the Wall to worship. When it became clear that he had become confused and couldn't make his way back, she solicited help from a man nearby. Before going to retrieve the husband, he scolded the woman for allowing him to go on his own. Not only was his timing inappropriate; the scolder was insensitive to the fact that the woman was prohibited from accompanying her husband up to the Wall and didn't have the option of bringing along another male to help her in this instance. — N.H.M.

Reproof should almost always be offered one-on-one. Offering reproof in a group, even a small group, will very likely lead to shame. Poorly delivered criticism can do enormous damage. — D.E.

Reproof should almost never be carried out via email. It is simply too impersonal a medium, and reproof is too important an activity to be carried out electronically. If phone or in-person meetings are impossible, the writer of the email reproof must be extremely careful to re-read the communication from the perspective of the person receiving it before sending it out. — S.J.G.

There is never a good reason to rebuke someone over email. When we send such an email, we're not really looking for a meaningful response. We're just hiding behind a convenient but deeply flawed intermediary. If the conversation is important and the *relationship* is important, then I will find a way to speak to the person in real time, no matter how difficult it may be. I have used email only to say to the person, "I am trying to reach you because there is something really important that I need to discuss with you" but not to share the content of my distress in the email itself. All the time spent reading and re-reading the content of an "email of reproof" would be better spent by picking up the phone and making the conversation a priority. — Y.R.

The notion that people are obligated to do *tokheha* is at odds with most of the conduct in contemporary American society. The attitude that you should "do your own thing" is widespread. Most people want to appear tolerant, nonjudgmental and open to a wide range of conduct. Jewish teaching recognizes that we have an obligation to help people improve, and that the community we live in will be profoundly affected by the conduct of its members. A rabbinic tale points out that the person on a boat who drills a hole in the bottom under his own seat affects everyone, and anyone on the boat has the right to object. (See the comment on Leviticus 19:18 in *Or Hahayim*.) Conduct should go without comment only if it causes no harm to individuals or the community.

Tokheha is often one of the few tools that can be used to challenge authority. If I choose to present *tokheha* in the form of a letter to the editor or a similar medium, I do so not because I necessarily believe *tokheha* itself will change the behavior. I do it because it will raise general consciousness and draw attention to the behavior that I find problematic. Perhaps this will increase pressure that over time could lead to behavioral change.   — D.J.L.

Tokheha has a salutary intent. Its goal, according to the Torah, is that we not incur guilt on behalf of the other. The goal of *tokheha* is to elevate our neighbor, not to humiliate her or him.   — R.H.

So much of the work of learning to speak skillfully is simply becoming conscious of what we say. Psalm 121 says, "The guardian of Israel (*shomer Yisrael*) never slumbers or sleeps." Our goal, then, is to learn to be *shomrim* for each other, or, as Rabbi Ira Stone puts it, to be awake to the needs of the other. Stone says that consciousness is another word for maturity. While being conscious does not mean we will always speak ethically or skillfully, we can learn that when we speak, we are always making choices and that we do so as *shomrim,* as guardians who are always in relationship to another in our care. One way to gauge whether our speech is skillful is to ask ourselves if what we say is in the service of the other.   — J.B.

It is easy for societies to develop in a dictatorial way that stifles creativity and freedom of thought. That would be profoundly problematical, and overdoing *tokheḥa* can have that effect. Therefore, it is critical to consider whether one is inappropriately attempting to reinforce a matter of personal taste or preference, or whether there is a genuinely significant issue at stake. Issues of morality and community conduct deserve careful dialogue to avoid a few sharp-tongued individuals taking the moral life of the community into their own hands. Values-based decision making is a useful method of tackling these questions in the community. (See the first book in the *Guide* for an explanation of this method.) The outcomes of these discussions can then provide guidance about which kinds of conduct should stimulate *tokheḥa*. It takes a community to create a moral climate.

A particular challenge of online communication is the lack of body language, intonation and other social cues that speakers use to convey tone and humor, and that recipients of speech use to provide cues back to the speaker about tact and appropriateness. Internet discussion groups are particularly prone to becoming "poisoned" by a few people who vocally and inappropriately critique others. At the same time, heavy-handed public intervention by a group moderator can make people afraid to express themselves for fear of being similarly reined in. As longtime moderator of an occasionally contentious Internet discussion group, I've found it best to begin with private *tokheḥa* to those who violate group norms of civility or confidentiality, and if public *tokheḥa* becomes necessary, to frame it as a public reaffirmation of group norms rather than a detailed blow-by-blow critique of an individual's behavior.   — M.F.

We rely too much on *tokheḥa* when we fail to sufficiently employ *haḳarat hatov,* positive feedback. Leaving aside the intrinsic moral appeal of celebrating righteous or laudatory action, positive reinforcement is often more effective than negative reinforcement.   — S.F.K.

Embarrassment, Apologies and Reconciliation

Tokheḥa done badly causes *halbanat panim* (literally, "whitening the face", but better translated as "shaming" or causing extreme embarrassment). Judaism has traditionally regarded it as a serious offense. The blood brought to the cheeks by embarrassment is said to remind the embarrasser that causing embarrassment is tantamount to shedding blood (Talmud *Bava Metsia* 58b). Certainly emotional injuries are as real as physical ones. There are many ways to humiliate, degrade and belittle people through the use of words. While *tokheḥa* is to be strongly encouraged, *halbanat panim* in any form is to be avoided unless it is necessary to avoid greater damage.

Rashi's commentary on Leviticus 19:18 teaches the connections between the intermediate phrase of the verse, "rebuke your counterpart" and the concluding phrase of the verse, "and bear not a sin on his account." Rebuke, but do so in a way that you do not incur sin by shaming the individual in the process.   — V.M.

An insult may not necessarily be obvious or intended. As a deaf person, I feel insulted when people imply that a communication accommodation such as a sign-language interpreter exists solely for the benefit of the deaf person. The reality is that communication accommodations are there for all parties involved, as they afford multiple parties an equal opportunity to communicate. I also feel insulted when people express the sentiment that spoken language is a higher form of communication than signed language.   — D.J.L.

In his book *Mesilat Yesharim* (chapter 20), Rabbi Moses Ḥayyim Luzzatto writes extensively about our duty *not* to do *tokheḥa* if it is likely to evoke a negative or rebellious response. He cites the talmudic instruction (B. Talmud *Yevamot* 65b) that "as it is our duty to reprove when we are likely to be heeded, so is it our duty to withhold reproof when we are not likely to be heeded."   — J.J.S.

There are many other ways to cause *halbanat panim*—
teasing, revealing secrets, commenting upon weaknesses,
public criticism and whispering, to name but a few. All
forms of *halbanat panim* are to be avoided unless they are
in the service of a greater good that cannot be reached in
another way.

Recognizing that one has hurt another person ought to
lead to making an apology and finding a way to make rec-
ompense. This process of *t'shuva* (moral return/repentance)
is not complete until one has done all in one's power to
undo the damage, but the verbal interaction that is part of
t'shuva is a critical part of the process. As a form of speech,
apologies are complex. They are not genuine apologies
unless they recognize the wrong that has been committed,

Attempting *tokheha* via a listserv is another form of *halbanat panim*.   — S.J.G.

As a deaf person, I often smile to myself when I read Leviticus 19:14—*lo tekalel
heresh,* "You shall not insult the deaf." Since Teutsch is positing a generic Jewish ethical position that one ought not to insult someone else, it becomes an interesting
question as to why the Bible singles out deaf people for "protection" against insults.
Maimonides argues that this biblical prohibition against cursing the deaf is actually
there to prohibit all cursing of any Israelite. He arrives at this conclusion by arguing
that by prohibiting the cursing or insult of one who *cannot hear, and therefore cannot
feel hurt,* the Torah is expressing its primary concern for those who would be doing
the cursing. A contemporary perspective on this argument clearly renders it
unsound and re-opens the question as to why the Torah specifically prohibits insulting a deaf person.   — D.J.L.

We are sometimes unaware of the subtle ways in which we have the power to
embarrass the people we love. In the *Al Het* on Yom Kippur, we atone for things
such as "impure lips, immodest glances and mockery" in recognition that a mere
look or casual comment can be devastating. Moshe Hayim Luzzato, in *The Path of
the Just,* cites R. Zakkai for great piety because he never even used a nickname to
refer to a friend.   — N.H.M.

acknowledge the damage done, make a commitment to repairing that damage, and express genuine regret. "I'm sorry you feel that way" is not an apology. Like *tokheḥa,* an apology is only effective when it is done with care.

Since sooner or later everyone hurts another person and since repairing relationships is a critical task in a family, work environment and community—indeed wherever people interact—making apologies is an important skill for practical reasons as well as moral ones. Genuine apologies rest upon confronting the pain caused and feeling regret about it. The promptness and sincerity of an apology have a major impact on its effectiveness. Humble, sensitive people generally have the easiest time apologizing; there is a complex interaction between *midot,* worthy traits of character, and the capacity to apologize. As in most forms of speech, caring counts.

Corresponding to the obligation to apologize is the obligation to let someone know that she or he has caused you to suffer. This too requires a gentle touch. You may have insulted me, but I am responsible for my response. Employing a judgmental or accusatory tone is, in essence, an insult in itself (requiring an apology), and it usually leads to escalation rather than healing. Better to say, "When you said (or did) that, it hurt me"; this is a non-aggressive way to invite an apology and to signal that the apology will be accepted. — J.J.S.

Once, I hurt a friend by one sentence. I hurt her deeply. I needed to really understand something about myself in order to see why I had said what I had said and why she had reacted so strongly. It is always painful to be that honest. The apology came from deep within me, and I have thought similar things again but never said them. Trust was broken in one sentence, but trust has been repaired through honesty and pain. — S.P.W.

Sometimes it is kinder to deliver an apology in written form in order to give the recipient time to absorb it. Before making an apology, it is important to consider whether, in certain circumstances, the apology will reopen a wound or cause pain for the other person rather than healing the rift in the relationship. — J.N.

Caring and speech also join together in the task of bringing people who are angry with each other back together. Reconciliation repairs rifts in relationships, heals tears in the human heart, and avoids rifts in a community.

The wisdom that "a healing tongue is a tree of life" (Proverbs 15:4) may be wiser than we ever knew! Recent research in neuroscience indicates that empathic connectedness and emotional nurturance stimulate biochemical changes in the brain that not only increase learning, but also can restructure neural architecture that promotes healing. This exciting new research offers a biological and neurological explanation for how and why the "talking cure," psychotherapy, works. It should also inform how we speak and communicate interpersonally in other contexts as well. Speech can literally be healing! Healing speech involves not only content, but tone of voice. Healing speech involves the creation of narratives that are not only egocentric but involve multiple subjective centers. The more complex a narrative is, the more neural network participation and integration between the right and left hemispheres of the brain will occur, increasing brain plasticity and empathic capacity. As professor of psychology Louis Cozolino writes: "The self is a matrix of learning and memory organized and encoded within hidden layers of neural networks" (*The Neuroscience of Psychotherapy, p. 170*). How we communicate, how we speak to one another and how we structure the stories we tell have the power to shape our brains, our selves and our communities!   — B.E.B.

Jewish tradition suggests that arguing (and we are an argumentative people!) can be done in either constructive or destructive ways. The school of Hillel and the school of Shammai—the two great rabbinical academies—argued for three years over a certain point of law. Finally, a voice was heard from heaven that announced both views to be "the words of the living God" (*Elu v'elu divrei Elohim ḥayim*), but the law was proclaimed to be in accordance with the view of the school of Hillel. Why, asks the Talmud, if both views are "the words of the living God," should the opinion of the Hillelites prevail over the Shammaites? The answer: "Because the disciples of Hillel were kind and modest; they taught both their own position and those of the school of Shammai; and they always cited with respect the opposing view before proposing their own." What a wonderful example for the contemporary Jewish community to follow, as we witness the increasing confrontation and alienation among religious factions in Israel and America. Is there just one correct opinion, or can more than one point of view represent "the words of the living God?" Can we accord one another respect; can we collaborate and compromise, without imposing one interpretation of the *halakha* or tradition over another?   — D.C.S.

Truly "a healing tongue is a tree of life" Proverbs 15:4). Inviting alienated people to a mediated conversation is the most direct intervention. Sometimes messages must be carried back and forth to prepare for that mediated conversation. The degree to which the message-bearer can legitimately exaggerate regret and hope for a reconciliation on the part of the two parties in order to get them into a conversation is a matter of controversy. However, it is clear that the message-carrier should certainly absorb negative feelings rather than pass them on so that the conversation starts as calmly as possible.

The midrash (*Yalkut Shim'oni* 2:583) teaches that when two people were angry with each other, Aaron, the first high priest, would tell each one that the other one was sick with remorse and wanted to make up. Of course, when they would then see each other, their hearts would soften, and they would make up. When I first learned this in grade school, I thought Aaron was lying, albeit for a positive reason. But now I see that he was actually telling the inner truth that the two people, blinded by their anger, could not see themselves. That truth is that each of them was longing to reconnect with the other. This is the truth of the human heart underneath all the protective devices we have developed. It is not lying to refer to that deep inner truth as the truth.   — V.M.

Promises, Oaths and Vows

One of the major purposes of speech is to find ways to cooperate for mutual benefit. Such efforts very frequently involve task division, an exchange of goods or an exchange of labor for goods. The vast majority of these arrangements are made orally, and only the most significant are reduced entirely to writing. Whether or not they are put in writing, these arrangements involve promises.

The foundation of the Jewish views on promises, oaths and vows is the concept of *brit,* or covenant. A covenant presumes the reliability and fidelity of the partners. Absent that, promises, oaths and vows lack a binding basis. — R.H.

Without diminishing the importance of following through on one's promises, there is also a danger of being too unforgiving when others do not follow through on promises made with the best intentions. "How could you have done that when you promised to do otherwise?" We are supposed to be little lower than angels, but we are also human and flawed, and we do not control everything in our lives. It is the other person's responsibility to keep his or her word; it is my responsibility to be forgiving. — J.J.S.

Consider the classic case of a promise given on her deathbed to the only other resident of a remote desert island. Some who focus on an action's consequences would say the promise is not binding: if the beneficiary is dead and no one ever knows the promise has been broken, there can be no bad consequences. I believe that the promise is binding because of an obligation to treat the other as an end, because of the virtue of truth-telling, and because of the qualities of character that are developed by promise-keeping. — S.F.K.

Consider the case of Franz Kafka, who extracted a promise on his deathbed that all of his unpublished writings would be burned. We are fortunate that Max Brod did not fulfill his promise to destroy Kafka's work but, in fact, went on to publish it posthumously. The world is richer for Brod's decision. — D.D.M.

Minor breeches of implied promises are sometimes unavoidable, but patterns of such breaches are a significant problem. It is part of a promise not only to do the things you say you'll do, but also to be where you say you'll be when you say you'll be there. Of course it is not always possible, but we should try to hold ourselves to these standards. — D.J.L.

People act based on those promises and suffer disappoint-
ment, frustration, and sometimes other forms of loss
when those promises are violated. When promises are reliable, cooperation is much easier, and the life of a community benefits. Because there is so much riding on them,
Jewish tradition understands oral commitments to be
binding.

Sometimes promises are made as a direct exchange. At
other times they are made as a favor or as a payment for
previous help. Altruism can also partly or wholly motivate
a promise or commitment. People have long memories
and complex motives, so the nature of the exchange is not
always obvious. Regardless of the motivation, once a
promise is made, it constitutes a bond that is binding
unless outside forces make its fulfillment impossible.

It is a high compliment to say of someone that her
word is her bond. Fulfilling commitments and promises

Sometimes the "character flaw" actually has a biological basis, as with people who
have Attention Deficit Disorder. The number of people diagnosed with ADD has
skyrocketed, in part because of changes in the way we do work that have resulted in
increased demands for organization and attention in a world full of information. A
diagnosis of ADD does not relieve a person of the obligation to act on promises. But it
can actually help the person learn to be more responsible as the person discovers that
his/her inability to carry out tasks in a linear fashion is not a "character flaw" at all, but
one based in difference. People attempting to help people who have been unreliable
should be aware of the biological source of the problem for some people.   — S.J.G.

The story of Jephthah's daughter (Judges 11) demonstrates that vows were considered
dangerous in biblical thought. While no one today would recommend following Jephthah's rigorous example of fulfilling a poorly constructed vow, the capacity of careless
oaths, vows and promises to lead to undesirable ends is still with us.   — D.E.

provides the currency on which agreements, partnerships, and teamwork rest. Clarifying expectations in advance and committing them to writing avoids conflicts later about the nature of the commitment, which is important for protecting all the parties to any agreement. Whether the context is family, community organization, workplace, or friendship, fulfilling promises and agreements builds trust and a willingness to do more together in the future. Individuals who are not trustworthy in this way lower the esteem in which others hold them and make them less likely partners in any undertaking. This unreliability represents a character flaw that tends to get worse with time unless the person receives help in making changes. *Tokheḥa* is important here!

As serious as vows are, an immoral vow may not be kept. Rabbinic Judaism created mechanisms for a rabbinic court (*bet din*) to release a person from a vow in some circumstances; a ritualized form of that release is familiar to many from the opening prayer of Yom Kippur, *Kol Nidre*. Rabbinic sources criticize Jephthah (Judges 11:30–40), who rashly vowed to sacrifice the first creature he saw at his home, which turned out to be his daughter. The rabbis criticize him for not seeking release from this vow. (See, for example, *B'reishit Raba* 60:3.).   — R.P.T.

Judaism regards vowing as a deeply serious commitment, one from which there is no turning back. But perhaps there are alternatives to the idea that a vow is only fulfilled by the "completion" of it. A vow points in a direction and names an intention. I think it is possible to treat "vow" as a verb, as a practice to live into, and not as a static noun. Norman Fischer writes, "When you vow, you get in touch with and give yourself completely to what matters most: the experience of receiving an inner calling and answering that calling with your whole life." Vows have the potential to bring us into the world with passion and conviction.   — J.B.

Oaths and vows (*nedarim*) are even stronger than promises. They go beyond conditional statements to being absolute commitments. This is why a traditional Jew agreeing to meet someone for dinner or bring something to a potluck might agree to do it while adding the phrase *b'li neder,* without making a vow. The person saying *b'li neder* has indicated intent that is binding only if no unexpected events, such as an accident or an illness, prevent meeting the commitment. A *neder* is made to God. It can be about a matter that is *beyn adam l'makom,* between an individual and God. For example biblical nazirites were individuals who made vows to abstain from such acts as consuming grape products and cutting their hair (see Numbers 6:1–23), such as Samson (Judges 13–16). A *neder* can also be *beyn adam l'ḥavero,* between one person and another. Every *neder* without exception is binding. For this reason the prevailing opinion throughout post-biblical Jewish history has been that people should be discouraged from making vows.

Frankness, Boasting and Vulgarity

Some people use oaths quite differently to provide emphasis to their speech, differentiate themselves from others, or create a rowdy tone. Invoking the name of God or using vocab-

Communal norms of speech evolve. Recent scholarship has increased awareness of the ways in which speech can be unfairly used to attain and assert power over other individuals or groups. This often involves labeling, in which certain forms of speech are associated with identities of gender, class or ethnicity. The power of this labeling can also be reversed by the people against whom such language is directed. For example, some gay men and lesbians have self-consciously and positively adopted the term "queer," effectively reversing its use in negative labeling. — R.H.

ulary to which holiness is attached for shock value degrades a precious part of language. Issues of gender, power and class are raised by inappropriate use of this language.

Another form of calling attention to oneself is boasting. While this may stem from personal insecurity, it often takes the form of exaggeration, which is a violation of truth-telling. Boasting frequently stimulates *l'shon hara* as a response, and rarely has the effect of bolstering the boaster, so it is best avoided. Paying honest compliments is a way of supporting people and strengthening interpersonal ties. Recognizing the accomplishments of others is a morally worthy undertaking.

We live in a time when we recognize the dangers attached to excessive modesty; we appreciate the freedom to explore sensually and sexually and to use language that supports this freedom and the diversity it engenders. However, there is a difference between that frankness and the vulgarity that cheapens language and demeans the people who use it. The challenge is to be both open and respectful when discussing sexuality and other topics that were once off-limits.

The flip side of boasting is false humility. Along with honest praise of others, we must learn to accept compliments and acknowledge our own achievements in a way that neither inflates nor diminishes our accomplishments. We find this lesson in the response to the compliment *yasher koah* (May you have continued strength). By answering *barukh tehiyeh,* may you be blessed, we are acknowledging our awareness of Divine presence and blessing in our lives. — N.H.M.

Contemporary stand-up comedians are extraordinary in their often excessive use of vulgar language. I often wonder exactly what their audiences find so amusing about their humor. Most of the time I simply wish that these comedians would take a lesson or two from Bill Cosby, who frequently has his audience rolling with laughter without resorting to using a single vulgar word in his act. — D.J.L.

Avoiding coarse speech in all its forms as a speaker and as a listener helps to improve one's personal experience, improve community discourse and reduce the commercial production of vulgarity. This awareness should lead to reflection about the nature of our exposure through popular culture and media. Our conduct and language serve as a model to others, and especially to our children. Finding the line between frankness and obscenity requires exploration and community discourse. This is a conversation that is often avoided because we are aware of the destructive repression of previous generations and because standards shift. Nevertheless, that discourse is worthy of our active engagement in familial, congregational and organizational contexts.

The coarseness of contemporary culture is pervasive. The degradation of language is perhaps the most significant factor in the reduction in respect for differences and for the people who represent them. The phenomenon of talk radio is a major contributor to the pollution of political discourse. The shrill, blunt and often cruel attacks of the hosts and callers on anyone who disagrees with them makes those who differ into "the enemy," someone to be destroyed rather than someone with whom one can have a discussion. — R.H.

Distinguishing "frankness" and "vulgarity that cheapens the language" seems an extraordinarily culture-bound enterprise. "Golly" (short for "God's Body") was at one time shocking, but its use today as an exclamation is a mark of prissiness. — S.F.K.

Sometimes we feel the need to share intimate experiences with close friends in private. A good friend knows how much can be revealed without causing a friend's discomfort. — J.J.S.

While I affirm the underlying sentiment, "coarse" speech is very difficult to define in our diverse, multicultural society. The norms for what is coarse and vulgar change rapidly and vary among generations living in the same household. As a speaker, I am able to choose words that, for my sensibility, are not disrespectful or degrading. As a listener, I am challenged to stretch beyond the familiar and to discern the speaker's intent, even if she or he uses words that I would not choose. — J.J.S.

Speech and Technology

The advent of printing had an enormous impact upon speech. For the first time, words could be disseminated across vast areas. Once promulgated, words in the form of books took on a life of their own. Generally this has been a wonderful thing because learning, reading and access to many aspects of culture have been immeasurably aided—first by printing and then by the Internet. The results of scientific research that used to take centuries to become known could, through printing, become available in months. Over the Internet, it spreads in a matter of days. The Internet supports easy, rapid communication for community organizing, combating propaganda and other laudable purposes, and it links individuals and groups who need to connect for personal or professional reasons in inexpensive and effective ways.

On the other hand, with the advent of printing, writers and publishers became responsible for violations of *l'shon hara* and *motzi shem ra* that were far more egregious in scope than anything that had gone before. Such low material became a basis for earning a living for the first time. Immoral speech as a form of livelihood, however, was just

---

When one is bound by confidentiality, great care must be taken to ensure that public discussion of confidential matters is shaped so as to remove all identifying characteristics of the people in question. A rabbi posting to his rabbinic listserv asking colleagues for help in counseling "my synagogue's president, who has a drug problem" has breached confidentiality. Even "a lay leader who is struggling with an addiction" may provide too much information if the listserv posting should become public. If the information is sufficiently sensitive, a message such as "I'd like to speak in confidence with a colleague who can provide advice about working with lay leaders with personal problems" is about as far as it is appropriate to go.   — M.F.

in its infancy then. Radio, records, tapes, CDs, television, email, the Internet, the Web, blogs—who could have imagined the avalanche of new forms that speech would take? The opportunities that flow from them and the moral problems they raise are truly without end.

The amount of *l'shon hara* and falsehoods available through the media is virtually unlimited. It is difficult to avoid if one is given to reading gossip columns, blogs or forwarded emails, watching reality shows and talk shows, or listening to talk radio. It takes significant discipline to ensure that one does not invade the privacy of others in these ways. Blogs in particular often talk about third parties who have not given permission for the disclosures. Technology has multiplied the speed and magnitude with which gossip can wreak havoc. The contemporary media can harden us so that without noticing we talk with our friends and acquain-

---

Other than gossip columns (which by definition carry gossip), none of these other media, based on the nature of the media, must necessarily deliver *l'shon hara* or *rekhilut*. Purveyors of *l'shon hara* and *rekhilut* are misusing these media through their choices of language and content. It is dangerous to confuse the problem of a particular message with its medium of delivery. It takes the focus away from those responsible and contributes to our feeling of being victims of our own culture. People can choose to limit themselves only to blogs and talk shows that model a healthy exchange of ideas and information. — S.J.G.

In the days of snail-mail, people often wrote angry letters to get things off their chests, but knew enough to drop the letters in a drawer for a few days rather than mailing them. The instant availability of the "send" button makes it possible to zip off rapid replies without the intervening time necessary for "light" to triumph over "heat." Once you have clicked the "send" button and your email is off in cyberspace, you no longer have any control over where the email might be forwarded or who might read it. Clearly all Internet communications should be composed with this in mind. — R.H./D.J.L.

tances in ways that further this destructiveness. Email and instant messages should never be considered totally private forms of speech. They can be made public intentionally or inadvertently with devastating effect. Of course list-serves reach so many people that they *are* public. When they contain confidential or personal information, this should be a matter of serious concern. Reading any of these communications is morally equivalent to listening to gossip. They should be deleted unread—and *tokheḥa* offered to the senders.

Email, instant messaging and the Web make it very easy to conceal one's identity (age, gender, etc.) or to appear to be someone else. The resulting deceptions range from painful, practical jokes to major frauds. Such deception involves lying that often does harm beyond the imagination of the perpetrator. Engaging in such behaviors toward a friend, family member, acquaintance or stranger is wrong both because it involves lying and because it is destructive in other ways.

The new media purvey hard-core pornography and tasteless expressions in unprecedented quantities. These media can provide a safer environment for sex workers, and one cannot become infected by a sexually transmitted disease over the

Paradoxically, the same technologies that have the ability to create anonymity also have the power to make things public. When using cell phones, text messaging and other forms of wireless communications, we should view ourselves as if we were broadcasting a radio program to which anyone with the right kind of radio receiver can listen.   — C.H-M.

There is something to be said for the safety provided by anonymous speech when it comes to issues of whistle-blowing about abuses of power, but in Jewish communities, as opposed to corporations or government, the risks justifying anonymous whistle-blowing seem comparatively small compared with the potential for abuse of anonymous rumor and innuendo.   — M.F.

Web, but the availability of pornography over the Internet carries its own dangers. Legal censorship has many pernicious effects, but choosing to avoid contact with these things is a sensible personal and communal choice. These media have a huge power to alter the sensibilities of those who watch or listen that is difficult to measure or guard against.

Technological advances also make it easy to violate copyright and trademark laws, taking the property of others without payment or significant likelihood of being caught. The most common of these thefts is downloading or copying music or video. Such thefts are sometimes rationalized by the high retail cost of these goods. With the exception of the pricing of necessities, however, it is the right of the

---

Many problems arise from the widespread availability of pornography through the Internet. Those prone to sex addiction are much more likely to succumb to it, given their ease of access. Children can accidentally or purposely view inappropriate material. Pedophiles are easily able to identify potential victims. We have not yet developed the necessary ethical and communal norms, nor have we satisfactorily met the technological challenges, to enable us to appropriately manage the changes brought by the Internet. Articulating the problems is a first step toward the solutions.   — D.E.

While a safer environment for sex workers is a laudable goal, it would be even better if we were able to eliminate the conditions that lead people to become sex workers and to purchase sex for money.   — D.E.

In a digital environment, the question of when downloading, viewing or copying is a violation of copyright is often quite complicated, and content providers often claim rights that exceed their actual legal entitlements. There is an obligation to obey the law, but not to exceed it. S.F.K.

A robust and growing public domain is essential to cultural development. With the repeated extensions of copyright by Congress, works dating after the mid-1930s have stopped passing into the public domain. This protects corporate profits for centuries but means that vast quantities of books and other materials from that era can't see the light of day, since they are out of print and their copyright holders cannot be located.   — M.F.

owner to set prices and the right of the potential purchaser not to buy. The frequency of this violation has led many people to accept it as normative. Making theft common does not make it less wrong. Downloading or copying in violation of copyright laws is wrong even if it is just for personal use and not for resale. Theft without reselling the goods is still theft.

One of the issues created by these new modes of communication is the ease with which one can violate privacy, manipulate or spread falsehoods, further obscenity and steal intellectual and artistic property while remaining unseen. This lack of direct contact insulates the writer, director, speaker and producer from the *tokheḥa* that might otherwise constrain their conduct. Censorship creates such powerful dangers of its own that it cannot effectively substitute for internal moral constraints. Public conversation about these issues is needed as a way to generate the missing *tokheḥa*. While such conversation may not directly affect the "speakers," it can have an impact on the "listeners."

Many of us have been witness to virtual sparring matches between two individuals or even a group of people on a listserv. In these cases people often seem emboldened to say things one cannot imagine they would actually say in person. Since the act of writing can be cathartic, in such cases one should consider writing something and then deleting it rather than sending it.   — D.J.L.

Many people have been hurt by online conversations that would have occurred differently had the parties been speaking directly. We should be careful about fitting the content of communication to the medium carrying it. One major improvement would be to use emails and Instant Messages only for communication devoid of emotional content. Traditionally posted letters (allowing the recipient greater control over when and where the message is read), the telephone and face-to-face discussions are better suited to conveying emotion.   — D.E.

For Further Reading . . .

The most important work about Jewish speech ethics is the Ḥofetz Ḥayim, a pietistic work replete with quotations from the Bible and rabbinic sources. Written in Hebrew, it has been partially translated into English, and many Orthodox authors have written derivative, simpler works. One example is *Taharas Halashon* by Zeev Greenwald, translated into English by David Landesman.

More contemporary Jewish approaches are taken by Joseph Telushkin in *Words that Hurt, Words that Heal* (William Morrow & Co., 1996) and Elliot Dorff in chapter four of *The Way into Tikkun Olam* (Jewish Lights, 2005).

The relevant sections of the Jewish codes are useful, as are articles in the Jewish encyclopedias.

There is also a substantial secular and legal literature. These include such books as *Lying* by Sissela Bok, *Legal Secrets* by Kim Lane Scheppele, and several books by Deborah Tannen.

For substantial discussions of visiting the sick, discussing impending death and comforting mourners, see *Beḥoref Hayamim,* published by the RRC Ethics Center.

Biographies of Contributors

JOSHUA BOETTIGER is a 2006 graduate of the Reconstructionist Rabbinical College.

BARBARA E. BREITMAN is a psychotherapist in private practice who teaches at the Reconstructionist Rabbinical College and taught at the University of Pennsylvania School of Social Work. She is the coeditor of *Jewish Spiritual Direction: An Innovative Guide from Traditional and Contemporary Sources.*

RABBI DAN EHRENKRANTZ is President of the Reconstructionist Rabbinical College and its Aaron & Marjorie Ziegelman presidential professor. A past president of the Reconstructionist Rabbinical Association, he previously was rabbi of Congregation Bnai Keshet in Montclair, NJ.

RABBI MICHAEL FESSLER is co-rabbi of Congregation B'nai Tikvah in Sewell, New Jersey. He moderates the listserv of the Reconstructionist Rabbinical Association.

RABBI SHAI GLUSKIN serves at the Jewish Reconstructionist Federation, where he has developed an expertise on learning and communication via the Internet.

CHAYIM HERZIG-MARX has served as interim executive director of the Jewish Reconstructionist Federation. He is a past board member and treasurer of JRF and a founder of Congregation Dorshei Tzedek in Newton, MA.

RABBI RICHARD HIRSH is Executive Director of the Reconstructionist Rabbinical Association and teaches at the Reconstructionist Rabbinical College. He was Editor of *The Reconstructionist* journal from 1996–2006.

LEAH KAMIONKOWSKI is a certified public accountant. A vice president of the Jewish Reconstructionist Federation, she is a member of Kol HaLev in Cleveland, OH.

TAMAR KAMIONKOWSKI, Ph.D. is the Vice President for Academic Affairs and Associate Professor of Biblical Civilization at the Reconstructionist Rabbinical College.

SETH KREIMER is the Kenneth W. Gemmill Professor of Law at the University of Pennsylvania and a past president of Congregation Mishkan Shalom in Philadelphia.

DARBY JARED LEIGH, M.A. is a student at the Reconstructionist Rabbinical College. He is a former Cooperberg-Rittmaster Rabbinical Intern who has written on ethical questions related to hearing impairment.

RABBI NINA H. MANDEL serves Congregation Beth El in Sunbury, Pennsylvania. She is also a lecturer in the department of Philosophy and Religion at Susquehanna University.

RABBI VIVIAN MAYER serves Congregation B'nai Israel in Danbury Connecticut.

DEBORAH DASH MOORE is the Frederick G.L. Huetwell Professor of History at the University of Michigan and director of the Jewish studies program there. She is a member of the West End Synagogue in New York City.

JOYCE NORDEN previously was an Assistant Professor of History at Carnegie-Mellon University and served as the Vice President for Institutional Advancement at the Reconstructionist Rabbinical College.

RABBI YAEL RIDBERG is the rabbi of West End Synagogue in New York City.

RABBI DENNIS C. SASSO is Senior Rabbi of Congregation Beth El Zedek and Affiliate Professor of Judaism at Christian Theological Seminary in Indianapolis, IN. He is a past president of the Reconstructionist Rabbinical Association.

RABBI JACOB J. STAUB is Professor of Jewish Philosophy and Spirituality at the Reconstructionist Rabbinical College, where he directs the program in Jewish Spiritual Direction. He previously served as RRC Vice President for Academic Affairs. He is the co-author of *Exploring Judaism: A Reconstructionist Approach*.

RABBI ROBERT J. TABAK is a chaplain at the Hospital of the University of Pennsylvania and editor of the RRA newsletter.

RABBI DAVID A. TEUTSCH is the Wiener Professor of Contemporary Jewish Civilization and Director of the Levin-Lieber Program in Jewish Ethics at the Reconstructionist Rabbinical College. A past president of the College, he was Editor-in-Chief of the *Kol Haneshamah* prayerbook series.

RABBI SHEILA PELTZ WEINBERG is Outreach Director and a staff member teaching meditation at the Institute for Jewish Spirituality. She has previously served as a congregational rabbi, Hillel director and community relations professional.

Index